LEGENDARY
LABOR LEADERS

PROFILES

Amazing Archaeologists and Their Finds
America's Most Influential First Ladies
America's Third-Party Presidential Candidates
Black Abolitionists and Freedom Fighters
Black Civil Rights Champions
Charismatic Cult Leaders
Courageous Crimefighters
Environmental Pioneers
Great Auto Makers and Their Cars
Great Justices of the Supreme Court
Hatemongers and Demagogues
Hoaxers and Hustlers
International Terrorists
Journalists Who Made History
Legendary Labor Leaders
Philanthropists and Their Legacies
Soviet Leaders from Lenin to Gorbachev
Top Entrepreneurs and Their Businesses
Top Lawyers and Their Famous Cases
Treacherous Traitors
Utopian Visionaries
Women Business Leaders
Women Chosen for Public Office
Women in Medicine
Women Inventors and Their Discoveries
Women of the U.S. Congress
Women Who Led Nations
Women Who Reformed Politics
The World's Greatest Explorers

LEGENDARY LABOR LEADERS

Thomas Streissguth

The Oliver Press, Inc.
Minneapolis

The Oliver Press, Inc.
Charlotte Square
5707 West 36th Street
Minneapolis, MN 55416-2510

Library of Congress Cataloging-in-Publication Data

Streissguth, Thomas, 1958-
Legendary labor leaders / Thomas Streissguth.
p.   cm.—(Profiles)
Includes bibliographical references and index.
    Summary: Traces the history of the labor movement in the
United States through brief biographies of labor leaders: Samuel
Gompers, Eugene Debs, William Haywood, "Mother" Jones, John
Lewis, A. Philip Randolph, Jimmy Hoffa, and Cesar Chavez.
ISBN 1-881508-44-7
1. Labor leaders—United States—Biography. 2. Labor movement—
United States—History. [1. Labor leaders. 2. Labor movement.]
I. Title. II. Series: Profiles (Minneapolis, Minn.)
HD8073.A1S77   1998
331.88'092'273
[B]—DC21   97-29017
                                    CIP
                                    AC

ISBN 1-881508-44-7
Printed in the United States of America

04 03 02 01 00 99 98   8 7 6 5 4 3 2 1

Contents

American workers can thank labor unions for a 40-hour workweek, a two-day weekend, and the minimum wage. In contrast, these 1929 strikers, like many laborers of the time, worked much more than 40 hours each week.

Introduction

*A*t the beginning of the nineteenth century, the young American republic was still largely rural. Owners of tiny shops and home-based businesses in small towns provided shoes, furniture, farm implements, and other goods and services that farmers and townspeople needed. But in the course of the next 100 years, cities grew and factories were built to manufacture these goods on a mass scale for people throughout the nation. Jobs in these factories or in mines owned by huge companies were a far cry from work on farms or in small shops. Poorly paid workers toiled for long hours in noisy or unsafe conditions.

Although major labor upheavals would not come until later in the century, workers soon began to demand better conditions. For most of the 1800s, strikes and petitions by laborers in factories or mines were scattered and usually unsuccessful. Many employers simply waited

Before labor unions gained power, it was not uncommon for workers, like these phosphate miners in Florida, to put in 12-hour days, six days a week.

until the striking workers were desperate to return to work—and then fired the strike leaders. Reforms did not come easily. The struggle to establish labor unions that could negotiate wages, hours, and working conditions was marked by violent strikes and bloody repression by employers, police, and even the U.S. government.

At first, labor organizations seemed to be losing their battle. Because of the large number of unskilled immigrants and southern blacks who poured into northern cities, employers could easily replace troublemakers with new workers. But as the United States found itself becoming a part of an international economy and facing two world wars, the nation grew more dependent on big industries and the automobiles, steel, rubber, and oil they produced. The mass of industrial workers found their collective voice growing stronger because strikes by workers in these industries could now shut down the nation.

As unions grew more powerful, labor leaders gradually expanded their vision of the labor movement. While early organizers had intentionally restricted their unions to white men in the skilled trades, unions now gained strength by organizing women, blacks, and recent immigrants. Activists also sought legislation to protect the right to form unions. Furthermore, laws improved workers' lives by establishing an eight-hour workday and a minimum wage, by banning child labor, and by enforcing safety measures in the workplace.

From the start, there were widely differing ideas about the goals of the labor movement. The eight leaders in this book had different opinions of what a labor union should be and what it should do.

In the 1880s, Samuel Gompers organized the American Federation of Labor (AFL), a national association of labor unions. The unions in what is now the American Federation of Labor-Congress of Industrial Organizations (AFL-CIO) include more than 13 million members, making the AFL-CIO the largest association of labor unions in the United States. But when Gompers was alive, many other labor leaders considered the AFL a mortal enemy. Rather than calling for radical social change, Gompers's philosophy of "business unionism" simply sought to get better wages, hours, and benefits for skilled workers.

The desire to change society radically drove Eugene Debs to found the American Railway Union (ARU). This

The employment of children in factories and mines was a growing problem in the late 1800s. By 1900, one in every five children under the age of 16 worked to help his or her family. This girl was a spinner in a Vermont cotton mill.

was one of the first *industrial unions*—unions that organized all workers in an industry instead of dividing them by their craft or trade. Someday, Debs hoped, these united workers would gain the power to take over whole industries. Although his union was destroyed, Debs went on to run for the U.S. presidency five times on the Socialist Party ticket.

"Big Bill" Haywood's union was based on a socialist philosophy similar to Debs's. The Industrial Workers of the World (IWW) sought to unite all industrial workers, with the ultimate goal of workers running governments and managing national economies. Haywood's IWW failed, but its radical vision opened workers' eyes to the possibility of a successful mass labor movement.

One of the leaders who was inspired by the vision of workers seizing power was Mary "Mother" Jones. Even as an elderly woman, she rallied miners to fight for better wages and conditions—with violence if necessary.

The head of the United Mine Workers (UMW), John L. Lewis, took a different approach. Rising to the top of the UMW as the IWW and the socialists were in decline, he became the strongest force in organized labor during the 1920s and 1930s. To help workers gain financial security during the Great Depression of the 1930s, Lewis collaborated with the administration of President Franklin D. Roosevelt to pass new federal laws protecting collective bargaining and union recognition by employers.

These new laws allowed A. Philip Randolph to win a victory for his Brotherhood of Sleeping Car Porters, the first and largest African American union. After 12 years of unsuccessful organizing, Randolph and his union finally defeated the Pullman Palace Car Company.

Like Randolph, Cesar Chavez faced the tremendous task of organizing a group of workers who had never been organized before. In 1962, Chavez created the United Farm Workers (UFW) for impoverished migrant farm laborers. Practicing nonviolence and protesting injustice by fasting, Chavez inspired people across the nation to boycott fruits and vegetables from nonunion companies.

Jones, Randolph, and Chavez lived in poverty while devoting themselves to their unions, but not all union leaders were so self-sacrificing. Jimmy Hoffa of the International Brotherhood of Teamsters formed a partnership with organized crime that allowed the Teamsters to grow into the largest and wealthiest single union in the nation's history. The corruption ultimately led to Hoffa's murder, and his abuses of power still affect the 1.4 million Teamster members.

Many unions, including the Teamsters, experienced phenomenal growth in the 1930s and 1940s. At the end of World War II in 1945, more than 35 percent of American workers were members of labor unions—the highest proportion in history. Since that time, union membership has gradually declined, dropping to less than 15 percent in the late 1990s.

There are many reasons for the loss of union members. Employment in mass-production industries has fallen as many businesses move their factories overseas to take advantage of lower labor costs. New laws prevent unions from requiring workers to join their ranks, and

These retail clerks in St. Paul, Minnesota, went on strike in 1949, when over 30 percent of U.S. workers still belonged to labor unions.

employers in many states have the right to hire workers to replace strikers permanently. Most workers in the fast-growing service sector—retail, food service, banking, trade, real estate, and insurance—do not join labor organizations because they see unions as the domain of factory and industrial workers. Increasingly, unions are viewed as obstacles to business success.

Nevertheless, labor unions survive. Many people even predict that unions are regaining strength. They point to the successful Teamsters strike that shut down United Parcel Service (UPS) for two weeks in 1997. The broad goals of the union in the UPS strike—to create full-time jobs paying decent wages and to increase workers' control over their pensions—were similar to the goals of the eight labor leaders in this book, whose stories still inspire millions of workers.

Samuel Gompers (1850-1924) declared, "I want to live for one thing alone—to leave a better labor movement in America and in the world than I found in it when I entered, as a boy, the . . . struggle for the right."

1

Samuel Gompers
Granddaddy of the Labor Movement

*T*he workday has begun on an upper floor of a New York City building. Workers at long tables sort through piles of dark brown leaves. As they work, they listen to a reader recite stories from the newspaper or they talk among themselves. With nimble fingers trained in long apprenticeships, they roll the tobacco into thick cigars.

Like these people, Samuel Gompers was a highly skilled cigarmaker. Born in England on January 27, 1850, Samuel was the oldest son of Solomon Gompers, a Dutch Jew who made cigars in East London. Samuel began learning the trade when he was just 10 years old. When

Like 10-year-old Samuel Gompers, these boys in Tampa, Florida, were rolling cigars instead of attending school.

Solomon saw that the field was becoming overcrowded, he decided to move to the United States in 1863.

The year after the Gompers family came to New York, Samuel joined the Cigarmakers Local 15, a union of English-speaking cigarmakers. When his workday was over, Samuel often attended lectures by socialist speakers or debated politics and labor problems with his friends.

In the late 1860s, Gompers and other cigarmakers suddenly found themselves competing with unskilled workers who used a new invention, the cigar mold. These "bunchbreakers" earned lower pay in the form of *piece rates*—a set fee for each cigar made. They worked in tenement apartments rented from their employers and shopped at *company stores* owned by their employers. These workers, many of whom were poor immigrants, were not unionized.

There was little unionized cigarmakers could do about bunchbreakers. Nor did they have a say in their own wages, hours, or working conditions. They could stop working, but with weak leadership and no strike funds to make up for lost pay, most strikes were failures.

Skilled cigarmakers' jobs and wages were threatened as long as employers could hire bunchbreakers for

Because bunchbreakers were paid by the number of cigars they made, whole families would stay up late into the night rolling tobacco.

less money. But the strict requirements for membership in the Cigarmakers International Union (CIU) prevented tenement workers from joining. In 1872, Gompers and his friend Adolph Strasser decided to take action by forming United Cigarmakers and accepting cigarmakers of any skill level, including women and immigrants. When the CIU finally granted this new Local 144 a charter three years later, Gompers was elected president.

To avoid the unplanned strikes that had been common among cigarmakers, Gompers and Strasser imposed a careful organizational structure on Local 144. Each of the local's *shops* of seven or more workers, the smallest units of organization in a union, voted by secret ballot whether to strike. Strikes by shops had to be approved by the local's leaders as well. When a strike was sanctioned, the local appointed a committee to oversee the walkout and distribute food and money to the workers.

At this time, workers were reeling from the effects of a nationwide depression that had hit in 1873. Gompers and Strasser both believed that unions should provide benefits such as unemployment insurance and sick pay to attract members. Even though the CIU resisted these proposals, Gompers and Strasser instituted them in Local 144. Once Strasser became CIU president in 1877, the organization gradually began to offer these benefits to all its members.

As the two leaders had predicted, membership in Local 144 skyrocketed when the union began providing unemployment insurance and sick pay. Gompers and Strasser also strengthened the CIU and all of its locals by

Adolph Strasser worked closely with Gompers to strengthen the Cigarmakers International Union.

coordinating strikes and by restoring funds to striking locals. With these changes, the CIU won better wages and shorter workdays for its members, even as a nation-wide movement for an eight-hour workday faltered.

In the 1880s, mechanization was changing not only cigarmaking but all industries. Small workshops disap-peared, and unskilled workers now ran huge machines to mass-produce items formerly made painstakingly by skilled tradesmen. Given these circumstances, Gompers realized that workers would only gain real strength when unions banded together to demand change. In 1881, he and other trade-union leaders created the Federation of Organized Trades and Labor Unions. An alliance of inde-pendent trade unions, the federation focused on lobbying

Congress for legislation such as child and women's labor restrictions, an eight-hour day, and safety requirements.

But Gompers believed this was not enough. Government regulations could not solve every problem when trade unions were so weak and skilled workers were losing their jobs. A strong national federation of unions could coordinate strikes and negotiations with employers as well as lobby for protective legislation.

One national labor union already existed. Founded in 1869, the Knights of Labor had evolved into a union of producers—skilled workers and owners alike—which sought to protect members' livelihoods against bankers, investors, and big business. But Terence Powderly, president of the Knights of Labor, was more interested in cooperative ownership by producers than in the concerns of laboring people. In fact, he opposed trade unions and strikes and instead proposed negotiated settlements for conflicts between employers and employees.

Despite the philosophy of the well-established Knights of Labor, many people in the skilled trades were joining the union anyway in the 1880s, seeking to create new trade unions within the Knights. These *dual unions* duplicated the work of existing trade unions and competed with them for membership. Gompers opposed the Knights not only for the sin of dual unionism, but also for the organization's antistrike policies. Without strikes, Gompers was convinced, workers would never have any real power to change their working conditions.

In 1886, when his federation was pushing for an eight-hour day, Gompers called for a *general strike*, in which all union members would walk off their jobs. Although their leadership opposed the eight-hour demand, many branches of the Knights of Labor joined in the strike. Unfortunately for the Knights, the movement for a shorter workday took an unexpected turn that would lead to the union's rapid decline.

On May Day, workers and union leaders held huge rallies in cities across the United States. These protests were uneventful, but two days later, on May 3, a violent confrontation between workers and police took place in Chicago. In response, a group of *anarchists* (people who oppose any form of organized government) called a mass meeting for the next day in the city's Haymarket Square.

For several hours, the Haymarket Square rally was peaceful, with speeches and songs. But when police tried to break up the meeting and disperse the crowd, a bomb was thrown into the square, killing one policeman and wounding dozens. In response, police fired into the crowd and killed several demonstrators.

The identity of the bombthrower was never discovered, but Chicago police arrested eight anarchists. The men were convicted of murder, and four of them were executed later in the year. The violence devastated the public image of trade unionists, with the Knights of Labor being depicted in the press as dangerous troublemakers because of their prominence in the labor movement.

Gompers used the turn of events to go on the attack. At a meeting of all trade unions held two weeks after the Haymarket Square riot, Gompers and his federation demanded that the Knights of Labor disband all of their

For many radicals of the late 1800s, the executions of the Haymarket Square anarchists proved that the government would stop at nothing to prevent workers from demanding their rights.

dual unions and stop using competing *union labels*, which were tags placed on goods made by unionized workers.

In December 1886, Gompers called a meeting of the Federation of Organized Trades in Columbus, Ohio. At this meeting, the organization was transformed into the American Federation of Labor (AFL). Elected as the group's first president, Gompers began traveling all over the country, organizing new trade unions and persuading hundreds of existing unions to become part of the organization. These *affiliates* remained independent and had the authority to organize and call strikes on their own.

Eventually, every national trade union, except for the large railroad unions, joined the AFL's ranks. Backed by the AFL's treasury and nationwide influence, many affiliated unions were able to negotiate for better wages and finally win the eight-hour day for their members.

Threatened by the AFL's growth, Powderly, the president of the Knights of Labor, sought to make allies in the Populist Party, which fought for the rights of farmers and workers against banks and big businesses such as the railroad companies. But the Populists lost the 1892 elections, and an economic depression in the next year brought a further decline in the Knights' membership and prestige. By the turn of the century, the Knights of Labor had virtually disappeared.

At the same time, Gompers's growing power allowed him to set policy almost singlehandedly for the AFL and the national trade-union movement. Although he had once fought to include unskilled workers in his small cig-armakers' union, Gompers now saw these workers as a threat to his skilled members. In spite of his idealistic claims that the labor movement should include women and blacks, he also failed to require member unions not to discriminate. Furthermore, Gompers opposed the immigration of unskilled and illiterate people to the United States, fearing that such immigrants would compete with AFL members for jobs.

One of Gompers's biggest and most controversial fights was with industrial unionists who wanted to organize workers according to industry (such as rubber, oil, or steel) rather than by their particular trade. Despite the opposition of labor leaders like Gompers, industrial unionism slowly gained strength. Meanwhile, Gompers

"Labor Conquers All," announced this Latin banner
that hung over an annual convention of the American
Federation of Labor. By the late 1800s, this
statement seemed to be coming true.

and the AFL were becoming increasingly conservative.
Gompers's "business unionism" favored the American
capitalist system, in which businesses and industries are
owned by individual people and investors. He thought
the best way for workers to advance themselves within this
system was by perfecting a trade or skill so that their
labor grew more valuable. Just as a business that had a
monopoly in a certain industry controlled the price of
the industry's products, Gompers believed strong labor
unions representing all workers in a given field would
have a monopoly on labor and thus would be able to
negotiate the best contracts for their members.

In the early years of the twentieth century, many labor leaders were at odds with the AFL's political and social outlook. Some were *progressives*, who wanted to break up and reform business monopolies. Others were *socialists*, who favored the overthrow of the capitalist system. Two leading socialists, Eugene V. Debs and "Big Bill" Haywood, saw the wage system as the equivalent of slavery because workers were utterly dependent on their employers for their livelihood. To the socialists, the only fair solution was to take companies out of the hands of investors and capitalists and place them directly under the control of the workers.

Gompers fought hard to keep proponents of these ideas out of his federation. Although he thought laws should restrict child labor, he believed that other labor issues, such as pensions, unemployment pay, and health insurance, should be negotiated directly between workers and employers—without government interference. Gompers, however, did oppose legislation restricting the rights of labor unions to seek better conditions. The Sherman Antitrust Act of 1890, for example, banned "conspiracy in restraint of trade." Courts were free to interpret strikes as just such a "conspiracy," and employers could ask the courts to stop strikers. Union leaders and members found themselves facing fines and jail time—sometimes only for speaking in favor of a strike.

Businesses took advantage of the Sherman Act to fight labor unions. Instead of negotiating with labor leaders, employers simply asked for *court injunctions*, or legal orders, to stop a threatened strike. With their newfound power, many companies also forced workers to sign *yellow-dog contracts*—a written promise not to join a labor union—as a condition of employment. Some employers used *lockouts*, closing their doors and shutting down operations in response to a threatened strike.

The law was tested in 1906 when the Buck's Stove and Range Company ordered its stove polishers to work a longer day. AFL's magazine, the *American Federationist*, called on members to boycott Buck's Stove products. In response, the company asked for an injunction against the AFL. Gompers defied the order and continued to ask members not to buy the company's stoves. Although charged with contempt of court, Gompers still managed to avoid jail when the president of the Buck's Stove company died and his successor dropped the case. But the Sherman Act remained in force.

Court injunctions began to weaken the AFL in the early 1900s. Unable to strike or boycott, workers saw little advantage in joining unions. Gompers finally decided to seek recourse in the political arena when the AFL's membership began to fall. In 1906, the federation drew up a Bill of Grievances and presented them to Congress and President Theodore Roosevelt. The bill requested an eight-hour day for all workers, an end to court injunctions, and strict limits on immigration. When Congress and the president rejected their demands, Gompers urged AFL members to work against antiunion politicians in the congressional elections that autumn.

For the next several years, the AFL fought an uphill battle against antilabor legislation. Yet popular support for labor unions and for business reform was growing. In 1912, seeking to create an ally in the White House, Gompers threw his support to Woodrow Wilson, the Democratic candidate for the presidency.

With the help of the AFL, Wilson won the election. Despite the fact that Wilson turned out to have only a half-hearted concern for labor issues, most of the AFL's major demands were met by the end of his first term.

Gompers continued to back Wilson during World War I, even becoming an international leader in the war effort against Germany. As Gompers had predicted, labor made substantial progress during the war. New laws recognized the right of workers to form unions and bargain collectively with employers. Pay increased, many companies established the eight-hour workday, and lockouts

Even though organized labor backed Woodrow Wilson (1856-1924) for the presidency in 1912 and 1916, Wilson had earlier opposed unions and prolabor legislation.

were banned. Strikes, however, were prohibited for the duration of the war.

The gains soon disappeared after the war's end in November 1918. Companies resorted to scabs and strike-breakers to fight the demands of their employees—who were still forbidden to strike. As a result, the AFL once again began losing members.

Gompers's organization also faced new challenges. The nation's economy was being transformed as national corporations opened huge factories employing thousands of unskilled assembly-line workers. Run by professional managers with little or no background as common labor-ers, these corporations were unsympathetic to unions and to the demands of wage-earners. But the aging Gompers stubbornly clung to the trade-union concept. He became even more hostile to the growing industrial unions and their leaders, calling them Communists and traitors. By the time of his death in 1924, Gompers and the trade unions in the American Federation of Labor were seen by many as obsolete institutions that were irrelevant to the needs of modern workers.

Yet Samuel Gompers had established what is still the most powerful labor organization in the United States. The AFL continued to play an important role in the labor movement even as industrial unions rose to power in the 1930s. AFL presidents who followed Gompers guided the organization into the future by discarding many of Gompers's policies. In 1955, this trend culminated in the AFL's merger with the Congress of Industrial Organizations (CIO), a federation of industrial unions.

AFL president George Meany (left) clasps the hand of Walter Reuther, Congress of Industrial Organizations president, as the two organizations join forces in December 1955.

Expanding its vision of the labor movement, the federation also slowly ended the exclusion of women and minorities. The membership of the AFL reached 13.6 million in 1997.

Explaining "I am for Socialism because I am for humanity," Eugene V. Debs (1855-1926) devoted his life to ending the "slavery of industrial work."

2

Eugene V. Debs
Socialist Worker

*I*t was April 1894. In the bustling, booming city of St. Paul, Minnesota, two men with little in common faced each other across a wide conference table. James J. Hill was a wealthy and powerful railroad baron; Eugene V. Debs was an outspoken labor leader. A costly strike among the railway men working for Hill's Great Northern Railroad had brought them together.

To put his trains back on track, James Hill had strikebreakers, law-enforcement officers, and many newspaper editors at his disposal. Eugene Debs, who sought to restore a wage cut Hill had made, could count only on the

The year before the American Railway Union strike, railroad magnate James J. Hill (1838-1916) had completed his Great Northern railroad line between St. Paul, Minnesota, and Seattle, Washington.

determination of the scattered members of his young and untested American Railway Union (ARU).

Hill was confident. Most unions at this time were no more than social clubs or mutual-aid associations. They had little bargaining power and almost no legal rights. To break a union, a railroad owner had only to divide his workers against each other—engineers against firemen, brakemen against maintenance crews. Debs and the ARU could be dealt with in the same way.

Debs, however, knew he could rely on workers who belonged to other railroad unions. Responding to Debs's call for solidarity, switchmen in the railyards were turning trains around backwards, and brakemen were standing idle, refusing to board the trains. The engineers who drove the locomotives were also willing to help the ARU. For the first time, railroad workers were united.

Debs also knew that mill and factory operators were losing business and pressuring Hill to settle. James Hill was a tough and determined man. When the Great Northern strike began, he was convinced he could beat the ARU. Eighteen days later, Hill realized he had met his match in Debs. He agreed to restore full wages on the Great Northern line, and the strike was over.

Eugene Victor Debs was born in Terre Haute, Indiana, on November 5, 1855. His close-knit family ran a grocery store and butcher shop and were avid readers. One of Gene's favorite books was Victor Hugo's novel *Les Misérables*. In that book, the poor people of Paris rebel during the French Revolution of the late 1700s. He admired the rebels' bravery and determination.

In 1870, Gene quit school to work for the Vandalia Railroad in a train-painting shop. For 50¢ a day, the boy scraped grease, dirt, and paint from locomotives. In less than a year, Gene landed a job as a fireman. He now earned $1 a night for the hard and sometimes dangerous task of stoking the fuel in the trains' steam boilers.

As a fireman, Debs probably knew about the new Brotherhood of Locomotive Firemen, which was formed in 1873 to provide medical insurance and death benefits for its members. That same year, when an economic crisis hit the nation, even the more established railroad unions were unable to prevent layoffs. Unable to find work in Terre Haute, Debs left for St. Louis, Missouri.

Working for the railroads demanded long hours in dangerous conditions. Thousands of men were killed and injured every year, mostly through accidents caused by fatigue and poorly maintained tracks and equipment. After seeing one of his coworkers killed on the job, Debs quit and moved back to Terre Haute, where he found safer work with a wholesale grocery company.

In 1875, the firemen's brotherhood chartered Vigo Lodge Number 16, a local union in Terre Haute. Even though he was no longer a railroad worker, Debs joined the union and was elected secretary. In addition to writing up the minutes of the meetings, Debs threw himself into organizing workers.

Less than two years later, railroad workers staged a general strike to protest a cut in their wages, but the action failed because of tremendous governmental and business opposition. With the railroad unions in tatters, Debs sought new tactics. Instead of striking, Debs called for negotiation between labor and management.

Debs was a popular figure in Terre Haute, where people admired his commitment to the railroad workers. In 1879, voters elected him to the office of town clerk. The next year, as the Brotherhood of Locomotive Firemen slid into bankruptcy, he accepted the post of national secretary-treasurer. Debs traveled from town to town, persuading former members to rejoin the union. He also called on brakemen, engineers, switchmen, and railroad shop workers to form their own unions.

By 1881, the railroads had recovered from the depression of 1873. The firemen's union was now out of

Government troops fire on strikers from the Baltimore and Ohio Railroad in August 1877. Debs feared that the nationwide strike would destroy the Brotherhood of Locomotive Firemen.

debt and counted more than 3,000 members. Debs's success prompted Indiana's Democratic Party to nominate him for the state legislature in 1884. Winning the election easily, Debs took a seat on the legislature's Railroad Committee, where he planned to write bills favorable to railroad workers.

Debs's proposed legislation included a new liability law that would hold railroads responsible for job-related accidents. Although his bill passed in the legislature's lower house, opponents changed it so much in the upper house that he withdrew his support of the measure. Angered by this political maneuvering, Debs took little interest in further legislative work.

After Debs left office at the end of 1885, he returned to union work. Over the next few years, his position on strikes would change. While he had opposed strikes in the interests of harmony between owners and employees, now he slowly became disillusioned with employers' motives. Although he hoped that an industrial union would be powerful enough to make radical actions, such as general strikes, unnecessary, Debs felt they were justifiable. Resigning from the firemen's brotherhood in 1892, he turned his energies toward the formation of a single industrial union of all railroad workers.

In the summer of 1893, Debs founded the American Railway Union (ARU). One of the first industrial unions in the United States, the ARU welcomed all railroad workers, no matter what their job was or how much they were paid. Debs's prestige among railroad workers helped the new union sign up more than 150,000 members and charter 465 locals during its first year.

But the financial panic in 1893 soon put the ARU to the test. Many railroad companies were forced into bankruptcy. Others merged into larger companies and cut expenses and wages in order to survive the hard times. Railroad workers had little chance of winning raises from employers. Most merely hoped to keep their jobs.

Then, in April 1894, James J. Hill, president of the Great Northern Railroad, cut wages for the third time in eight months. The ARU threatened to strike if wages were not restored to their former level. Hill refused. Claiming the ARU did not represent his workers, he requested federal troops to stop the walkout.

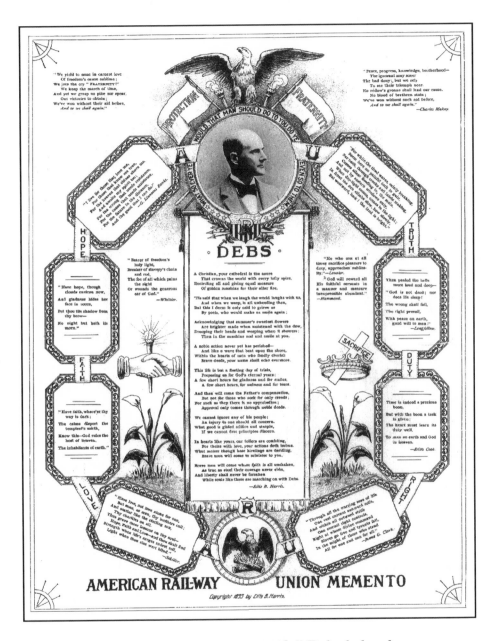

"Labor can organize, it can unify," Debs declared as
the ARU was forming its first locals in 1893. *"This
done, it can demand and command."*

Debs's membership drive and call for a general strike were so successful that he effectively closed down Hill's railroad. Great Northern engineers left passengers stranded in the middle of the northern plains. Switchmen abandoned the company's locomotives in railyards and in the roundhouses where they were parked. The following month, Hill backed down and granted the ARU's wage demands. Debs had won his first strike.

The victory brought Debs national attention as newspaper headlines announced the end of the strike. In the summer of 1894, new members were joining the ARU at the rate of 2,000 every day. The one-year-old union had become the largest in the nation.

Soon after the Great Northern victory, Debs and the American Railway Union faced a larger and tougher opponent in the Pullman Palace Car Company, a manufacturer of railroad sleeping cars. Most of George Pullman's employees lived in the company town of Pullman, near Chicago, Illinois. They worked long hours for low wages, which they were forced to spend on company-owned housing and in company-owned stores. Needless to say, the firm banned unions. But after Pullman cut wages and laid off employees in November 1893, workers formed a grievance committee to demand that their old salaries be restored. When the company fired three members of the committee the following May, workers walked off their jobs. Some of them traveled to Terre Haute to ask Debs's union for help.

Debs knew that in order to have any impact on Pullman he would have to call for a massive *sympathy strike* among railroad workers employed by other companies. Unsure the ARU could succeed, he asked Pullman to go into arbitration. The company refused.

In June, ARU members voted unanimously to boycott Pullman cars by refusing to work on trains carrying them. Over 100,000 railroad workers joined the protest. Hundreds of Pullman cars were separated from trains and left idle. The boycott quickly spread, bringing the nation's passenger-train system to a halt west of Chicago.

In early July, the government reacted by issuing a court injunction against Debs and sending a regiment of army troops to Chicago to put down the strike. Although prolabor Illinois governor John Altgeld strongly protested

U.S. troops patrolling by train prepare to put down the Pullman strike in Illinois.

this action, President Grover Cleveland claimed bringing in troops was necessary to end illegal interference with the U.S. mail, which was delivered by these trains. Fighting broke out in Chicago's railyards as troops charged strikers, killing more than 30 of them.

The court ruled Debs had violated the Sherman Antitrust Act of 1890, which sought to prevent "restraint of trade" by companies or individuals conspiring to fix prices or gain a monopoly over markets. Because courts held that the act also applied to unions that restrained trade by threatening or carrying out strikes, Debs was arrested and indicted for conspiracy to obstruct trade as well as mail delivery. Compounding this setback, Samuel Gompers, president of the American Federation of Labor (AFL), asked his own members who were striking in sympathy with the Pullman workers to return to their jobs. Without AFL support, the strike was crushed.

Sentenced to six months in jail for defying the no-strike injunction, Debs had a lot of time to think about what had happened. He saw the failure of the Pullman strike as proof that the courts and the government were in league with the railroad companies and other powerful employers. While in prison, he read the works of many socialist authors, who advocated public ownership of industries and the abolition of the capitalist system. Inspired by their theories, Debs enthusiastically adopted socialism not long after he left prison in 1895.

Debs soon became a leading socialist speaker. At the final ARU convention in 1897, he established a new socialist party, Social Democracy of America (SDA). In addition to calling for public ownership of key industries, Social Democracy planned to build an independent workers' colony in which laborers would own and manage basic industries. This colony would serve as a model for a nationwide socialist commonwealth.

But in 1898, Debs resigned from the SDA. He had decided to concentrate on promoting prolabor legislation and union organizing rather than a utopian scheme. Diving into politics, he ran for president in 1900 as a candidate of the new Social Democratic Party (SDP), formed by former SDA members. In the election, Debs

Debs accepted the nomination for president reluctantly because of poor health, but he threw himself into the campaign to offer voters a socialist alternative.

polled close to 100,000 votes—more than twice as many as any previous socialist candidate for president.

Encouraged by Debs's showing, several socialist factions united in 1901 to found the Socialist Party of America. This party nominated Debs as its presidential candidate in 1904. In that election, he polled just over 400,000 votes—about three percent of the popular vote. To many, Debs and the Socialist Party seemed to be the wave of the future. Socialist Victor Berger was elected as a congressman from Wisconsin, and cities from Schenectady, New York, to Findlay, Ohio, had Socialist

In 1908, Debs (with baby under the "R") campaigned for president from his "Red Special" train. This "whistle-stop" tour earned him 420,000 votes, 20,000 more than in 1904.

mayors and city council members. By 1912, hundreds of Socialists had been elected to office in the United States.

In that year, Debs was nominated as the Socialist presidential candidate for the fourth time. Americans were eager for reform, and Debs drew nearly 900,000 votes, making him the most successful socialist candidate for president ever. Following the election, Debs continued to travel throughout the United States, giving speeches and attempting to bring together the leaders of the various socialist factions.

Debs ran afoul of the government after the outbreak of World War I in August 1914. Debs and other socialists believed the war was a conspiracy of business and government to exploit the working classes. Capitalists and industrialists, they claimed, were using the conflict to profit from defense contracts. When the United States finally entered the war in 1917, the government passed sweeping laws to silence criticism. The Espionage Act made public speeches against the draft and the war effort illegal. Federal agents raided Socialist offices throughout the country, shutting down several newspapers and arresting party members. Debs became a prime target of the U.S. Justice Department.

In June 1918, Debs accepted an invitation to speak to a Socialist convention in Canton, Ohio. Even though he knew he risked arrest, he spoke out defiantly against the war. On the basis of this speech, Debs was indicted two weeks later for inciting resistance to the United States government. He was jailed for this offense on April 13, 1919—five months after World War I ended.

Debs's jail term did not prevent him from again running for president in 1920. His Socialist followers believed the campaign would focus national attention on Debs and pressure the government to free him and other political prisoners. Instead of making speeches on the campaign trail, Debs wrote a weekly 500-word article that was published and distributed by the Socialist Party from its headquarters in Chicago. In his articles, Debs

Debs was depressed as he campaigned from prison in 1920. "The people can have anything they want," he wrote. "The trouble is they do not want anything. At least they vote that way on election day."

continued to criticize the system of "wage slavery" and the positions of his major opponents in the presidential race, Republican Warren Harding and Democrat James Cox. Harding won the election, but Debs polled his largest number of votes ever—almost 920,000.

Despite its strong showing, the Socialist Party had been greatly weakened by government raids. Debs and more than 100 other opponents of the war were still in prison, and many other protesters had been deported from the country. The party eventually dissolved, and many of its former members joined the Communist Party.

Just before Christmas in 1921, President Warren Harding granted amnesty to Debs after the Socialist leader had served more than 2 years of his 10-year sentence. During the next few years, Debs worked to unify the different socialist factions. He also fought for the release of all political prisoners, improvements in prison conditions, and famine relief for people in the Soviet Union. His prison experience inspired him to write *Walls and Bars*, which was published in 1927.

Debs died on October 20, 1926, before he could see his book in print. He was still a widely popular labor leader. Ever since his days with the small and struggling railway unions, he had sought to improve working conditions and wages and had seen his political work as a means to that end. The respect he commanded, even from those who opposed his policies, focused attention on labor issues and helped to make a reality of many social reforms of the early 1900s.

Willing to do whatever it took to seize power for workers, the imposing William D. "Big Bill" Haywood (1869-1928) scoffed, "I despise the law."

3

William D. "Big Bill" Haywood
One Big Union Leader

*O*n a spring day in 1928, a funeral procession wound through the streets of Moscow, stopping at a small cemetery at the base of the Kremlin wall. The cemetery was reserved for heroes of the international socialist movement. To ensure a decent standard of living for workers everywhere, these heroes had fought for public ownership of all industries. Only one American rested there: John Reed, a journalist who had written a famous eyewitness account of the 1917 Russian Revolution, *Ten Days that Shook the World*. Joining Reed that day was an American labor leader named William D. "Big Bill" Haywood.

The man who would dream of helping to incite a worldwide workers' revolution was born in Salt Lake City, Utah, on February 4, 1869. His father, a miner and Pony Express rider, died when Bill was only three years old.

At the age of 16, Bill left home and drifted from mine to mine in the West for several years. He was a "hard-rock" miner, who dug gold, silver, and copper ore from veins deep beneath the mountains. Miners were paid as little as $1 a day to extract the precious metals with picks, shovels, and dynamite. Their hours were long— and their lives were usually short.

In the mid-1890s, when he was working in Silver City, Idaho, Haywood began to take an interest in the labor movement. Ed Boyce, the president of the Western Federation of Miners (WFM), met the young miner and convinced him to help organize a new WFM local union. The WFM had been founded in 1893 after a strike at a mine near Coeur d'Alene, Idaho. Impressed with Boyce, Haywood signed on, and WFM Local 66 was formed on August 10, 1896.

Then Haywood injured his hand while mining. Unable to work, he turned to organizing full time and also became the local's treasurer. Haywood signed up hundreds of new members, promising to gain better wages and working conditions. Soon Local 66 had won a *union shop*—which required all miners to become union members—and union-scale wages in Silver City mines.

The WFM sought better conditions for miners, but the union's broader goals were becoming revolutionary. Open to women and men of all races and ethnic groups,

Two decades after the 1849 discovery of gold in California, hard-rock mining had become an industry in the West. These Nevada copper miners worked pit mines (right) with heavy machinery.

as well as workers in any field, the WFM called for public ownership of industries and control of government by the workers. Haywood, who had adopted these socialist principles, became one of the WFM's most successful organizers. In 1898, the members of his local elected him as a delegate to their annual convention. Two years later, Haywood became the president of Local 66. Then, in 1901, he moved to WFM headquarters in Denver, Colorado, to serve as the union's secretary-treasurer.

The radical WFM had astounding success organizing during the first few years of the new century. By the end of 1903, the 10-year-old union had close to 40,000 members. But the WFM would soon confront the power of government and big business.

While Colorado's hard-rock miners were unionized and enjoyed decent wages and an 8-hour day, laborers at the smelters and mills that processed the ore worked 10 to 12 hours a day for much lower wages. In 1902, the WFM decided to organize these workers. Naturally, owners of the smelters and mills disagreed. The manager of the Standard Mill in Colorado City fired workers as fast as they joined the union.

The WFM retaliated with strikes against Colorado City refineries in February 1903. The other mills came to an agreement with the union, but Standard stood firm. Six months later, when the WFM started a sympathy strike at Cripple Creek mines to support the Colorado City workers, a virtual civil war spread across the state.

This time, the full power of the government was unleashed against the union as the state militia put down the strike. Over the next year, strikers were arrested and deported. "Big Bill" Haywood, as he was called by admirers, was beaten and jailed. Not only did the Cripple Creek strike fail, but by June 1904 all of the WFM's Colorado locals were also wiped out.

As a result of this strike, Haywood soured on the American government and became a committed socialist. Realizing that all mining-industry workers needed to band together, he also dedicated himself to industrial unions. To him, the traditional division of the labor movement into hundreds of different trade unions was a losing strategy. He believed that a single union, representing all workers, was necessary to combat the power of the state and big business. Such an organization would be much more effective in calling general strikes and forcing employers to bargain in good faith with their employees.

In June 1905, Haywood joined with WFM leaders and other union radicals, including Eugene Debs and Mary "Mother" Jones, to organize just such a union: the Industrial Workers of the World (IWW). What they called the "Continental Congress of the Working Class" met in Chicago to form an organization to counter the conservative probusiness policies of Samuel Gompers's American Federation of Labor (AFL). At the convention, Haywood announced, "We are here to confederate the workers of this country into a working class movement." Instead of seeking small gains for themselves, IWW members would work towards "the emancipation of the working class from the slave bondage of capitalism."

The "Wobblies," as the members of the IWW were called, wanted workers to destroy the capitalist system and seize control of industries. To meet these goals, IWW leaders sought "to organize the unorganized," especially unskilled manufacturing workers and migrant farm laborers. The Wobblies favored the general strike and direct actions such as sabotage, boycotts, and work slowdowns to interfere with production. Unlike most trade unions, they also accepted men and women of all races, ethnic backgrounds, and skill levels into their ranks.

Because it called for revolution, the IWW quickly became hated by both employers and the government. Business leaders and politicians searched for a way to shut the union down. On December 30, 1905, Haywood's opponents found grounds to attack him.

That day, in Caldwell, Idaho, a homemade bomb killed Frank Steunenberg, the state's retired governor. Haywood and Steunenberg had clashed in 1900 over a bitter strike in the Coeur d'Alene area. Now Haywood's old enemy had been murdered. The killer, Harry Orchard, was soon arrested, but many people suspected a conspiracy. Detectives began to investigate Orchard's possible connections with the WFM.

Promised leniency by his interrogators for talking, Orchard fingered Haywood, WFM president Charles Moyer, and former WFM official George Pettibone as the brains behind Steunenberg's murder. He also confessed to several other killings, claiming they had all been carried out on instructions from the WFM.

Idaho's governor requested extradition of the three WFM leaders from Colorado. In Denver, police seized Haywood, Moyer, and Pettibone and threw them into jail. Prevented from seeing their lawyers, the three men were hustled aboard a train early on the morning of February 18, 1906, and secretly transported to Idaho.

The three defendants were refused bail and sat in prison for more than a year. When Haywood's trial finally opened in May 1907, journalists jammed the courtroom. Prosecutor William Borah described the accused men as dangerous anarchists, pointing to the many WFM-led strikes that had turned mining camps into battlefields. But Borah had only Orchard's testimony to support his charge of conspiracy to murder Frank Steunenberg.

Haywood (standing) with fellow defendants Charles Moyer (right) and George Pettibone outside the Boise, Idaho, sheriff's office in 1907

The WFM had hired Clarence Darrow, the nation's leading defense attorney, to represent the three men. Over the next few weeks, Darrow easily proved that Orchard could not have committed all of the crimes to which he had confessed. Orchard was shown to be an opportunistic liar, and Haywood was acquitted.

Haywood took full advantage of his new celebrity to cast himself as the leader of the socialist movement. Charles Moyer, on the other hand, had been deeply frightened by the trial. Distressed by his reputation as an anarchist, he sought to be seen as a responsible labor leader who was willing to work with the mine owners instead of opposing them. Much to Haywood's disgust,

Moyer's WFM gradually turned more conservative. In April 1908, the WFM fired Haywood from his position as secretary-treasurer. Having left the IWW late in 1907, the union affiliated with the more moderate AFL.

Haywood now turned his energies to the Socialist Party. During the 1908 presidential election, he rode the "Red Special" campaign train with Socialist candidate Eugene Debs. Seeing Haywood's celebrity as an important asset, the Socialist Party of America (SPA) elected him to its executive committee in 1911.

That same year, the socialist dream of a government of industrial unions led Haywood back to the Wobblies. The IWW had gone through many changes and was rededicating itself to organizing nonunion workers. Meanwhile, Haywood was becoming frustrated with the SPA's faith in the political process. "No socialist can be a law-abiding citizen," he fumed. "It is our purpose to overthrow the capitalist system by forcible means if necessary." Most SPA members, however, now sought to make an alliance with the AFL.

Haywood had returned to the IWW on the eve of its greatest success—a textile workers' strike in Lawrence, Massachusetts. Mill operators had cut wages in response to a Massachusetts law reducing the legal working week from 56 to 54 hours. The wage cut sparked a spontaneous strike that in January 1912 soon spread to mills throughout the city. Because they were immigrants, the Lawrence workers were not welcome in the conservative AFL-affiliated United Textile Workers union, so they turned to the IWW for help.

Confrontations between police and strikers in the streets of Lawrence became violent. After a policeman was stabbed and a woman on strike was shot and killed, IWW leaders were arrested and charged with murder.

Under Haywood's leadership, striking workers organized drives to collect food and money and set up relief committees among the city's immigrant groups. But the strikers' most successful tactic was sending the children of textile workers out of harm's way to live with families in Pennsylvania, New Jersey, Vermont, and New York.

While most labor actions in the United States had been carried out by workers of a single ethnic group, under the leadership of the IWW, strikers in Lawrence united despite their different languages and religious beliefs.

The plight of the workers' children gained widespread public sympathy, and newspapers condemned the factory owners. So the owners finally decided to negotiate with the union. On March 12, workers were granted raises, overtime pay, and job security. Haywood and the IWW had scored an important victory.

The Lawrence strike brought the IWW further support from immigrant workers but increasing opposition from moderate Socialists. The IWW's image as a dangerous anarchist group was harming the SPA's chances at the polls. A new amendment to the SPA constitution expelled people advocating violence and criminal activity from the party—a provision aimed directly at Haywood and the IWW. In February 1913, the SPA leadership ousted Haywood from the party's executive committee.

Just after Haywood was kicked out of the SPA, 25,000 Paterson, New Jersey, silk-mill workers walked off their jobs when mill owners increased the number of looms each worker had to operate. On March 5, 1913, Haywood arrived to lead the strike.

This time, the suffering of the children failed to stir the public, so the IWW planned a performance in New York City. On June 7, workers marched out of Paterson toward the city. In Madison Square Garden, strikers from Paterson acted out incidents from the strike, dramatized a mass funeral to symbolize the workers' struggle, and sang the socialist anthem known as the "Internationale."

The exhibition was widely covered by New York's newspapers, but the Paterson strikers were starving after four months without a paycheck. The strike foundered by the end of July as disheartened workers gradually returned to the mills—without having gained any concessions.

The Paterson strike was one of several defeats for the IWW that year. A rubber strike in Akron, Ohio, and a strike against the Studebaker auto company in Detroit, Michigan, had also failed. But in May 1914, Haywood's leadership earned him the post of IWW general-secretary.

The financially strapped Wobblies needed more members, so Haywood coordinated a new organizing effort that began with western miners, timber workers, and farm workers. Then, in the summer of 1915, Haywood helped to set up the Agricultural Workers' Organization (AWO) to organize thousands of agricultural workers in the Midwest. Many of these workers were migrants who followed the harvests from state to state as the seasons changed. By the autumn of 1916, the AWO counted over 20,000 members—more than the IWW's total membership at the end of 1913.

The execution in 1915 of popular IWW songwriter Joe Hill on a questionable murder charge and a 1916 massacre of Wobblies in Everett, Washington, gained sympathy for the union. In 1917, after Haywood shifted the union's priorities away from revolution and toward better wages and working conditions, IWW membership hit 100,000. At the same time, factories ran at full capacity as the United States prepared to fight in World War I. Labor was in high demand, so unions were able to win better pay and working conditions for their members.

Although most labor leaders had agreed not to strike as long as the war lasted, the IWW and Haywood instead

In this 1917 cartoon, Minnesota forces of "law and order" try to root out the IWW, which sought to "conquer the world for the working class."

called for increased organizing and more strikes as the U.S. entered the war against Germany. Openly antiwar and antigovernment, Big Bill Haywood was once again public enemy number one. Many Wobblies wanted to use a general strike of IWW members in all industries to shut down the nation and stop the war.

58

IWW-led strikes against copper and lumber companies slowed down production of needed war supplies in the summer of 1917. That July, county militia rounded up 1,200 striking Wobblies in Bisbee, Arizona, and forced them to board a train for New Mexico, where they were left to fend for themselves in the desert. Antiunion vigilantes attacked IWW organizers, and IWW leader Frank Little was lynched that August in Butte, Montana.

Journalists and legislators painted Haywood and the IWW as traitors in league with Germany. Determined to stamp out the supposed treason, the U.S. Congress passed the Espionage Act, which made it a crime to impede the

Despite Haywood's threat of a general strike if the striking copper miners were not allowed to return to their families in Bisbee, President Wilson did nothing to help these victims of vigilantes.

war effort. Publicly criticizing the government or the armed services became serious offenses that were punishable by heavy fines and long prison sentences.

Using these new laws to justify his action, President Woodrow Wilson ordered a special investigation of the IWW. On September 5, federal agents raided the union's offices throughout the country. The government indicted 166 IWW members and leaders, charging them with conspiracy to incite opposition to the draft, impede wartime production, defraud employers, and violate employment contracts. Haywood spent more than four months in a Chicago jail before being released on bail in February 1918. Although Haywood offered to stop criticizing the war effort in return for having charges against all IWW members dropped, President Wilson was determined to destroy the union and turned down the deal.

The trial of 101 IWW defendants got underway in federal court in April. The scanty evidence—letters, pamphlets, and speeches—was good enough for the jury. In August, the Wobblies were found guilty on every one of more than 10,000 charges. Haywood received a 20-year sentence and was shipped to the federal penitentiary at Leavenworth, Kansas. Released on bail in July 1919, he prepared to appeal his convictions.

The government's actions had eliminated the entire IWW leadership. For the next few years, Wobblies struggled with appeals and legal bills. Even though workers were striking in record numbers across the nation, membership in the union plummeted in 1919 when many states made joining the IWW a crime.

In October 1920, the U.S. Circuit Court of Appeals upheld Haywood's charges. But instead of serving out his 20-year term, Haywood went into hiding. On March 31, 1921, he stowed away on a ship bound for Russia.

As a martyr of the workers' movement, Haywood enjoyed a hero's status among the new leaders of the Soviet Union. At the Soviet government's request, Haywood helped to build a steel plant and a coal-mining operation at a new industrial colony in the Ural Mountains. The former labor leader recruited engineers and laborers from the United States for the project, but the few who agreed to come soon returned to the United States, unable to bear the harsh Siberian weather. Haywood, too, resigned from the project in May 1923 and moved into an apartment in Moscow.

Unhappy in the Soviet Union, Haywood tried unsuccessfully to find a way to return to the United States without going to prison. As the 1920s wore on, Soviet officials turned away from the ideals of their workers' revolution. The new governing class held tightly to power, ruthlessly punishing those who were labeled enemies of the state for opposing official policies.

As his eyesight and health failed, Haywood became depressed. On May 18, 1928, a stroke killed Big Bill Haywood. According to his last wishes, he was cremated, and his ashes were divided between the tomb at the Kremlin wall and a cemetery in Chicago. There he lay at rest near a memorial to the most famous labor martyrs of an earlier generation—the four anarchists who were hanged after the 1886 bombing in Haymarket Square.

Famous for her battles with mine owners, Mary "Mother" Jones (1830-1930) warned, "There are no limits to which the power of privilege will not go to keep the workers in slavery."

4

Mary "Mother" Jones
Miners' Angel

Mary "Mother" Jones was not a miner, a mill worker, or a farm hand. She headed no unions and ran for no public office. Jones probably wouldn't have even claimed to be a labor leader. She called herself a "hell-raiser."

Future hell-raiser Mary Harris was born in Ireland on May 1, 1830. Her father, Richard Harris, was a tenant farmer who rented his land from a British landowner. Like other tenants, Harris paid his rent with a portion of his annual crop harvest. When crops were poor or failed, millions of Irish families suffered poverty and hunger. Mary's grandfather had been hanged for rebelling against the British rule of Ireland. Threatened with imprisonment for his anti-British views, Richard Harris fled the country. By 1838, he had earned enough money to bring his family to join him in Toronto, Canada.

Mary moved to the United States when she was a young woman and made her living sometimes as a schoolteacher and sometimes as a dressmaker. While teaching in Memphis, Tennessee, she met and married an ironworker and union member named George Jones in 1861.

Mary gave birth to a son and three daughters in quick succession. Then, in 1867, an epidemic of yellow fever struck Memphis. Within a few days, her husband and four children fell ill and died.

Mary Jones buried her grief as she helped nurse other yellow-fever victims in Memphis. Then she left her painful memories behind and moved to Chicago, where she again took up dressmaking to support herself. Working for the wealthy, she was troubled by the sight of homeless and jobless people in the city's streets. When a devastating fire ravaged the city on October 8, 1871, 90,000 Chicagoans joined the homeless population. With her house and dressmaking shop destroyed, Jones also found herself in the streets.

One day, while helping with the fire relief effort, Jones wandered into a Knights of Labor meeting and made her entry into the labor movement. She soon befriended Terence Powderly, a Knights of Labor leader, after sparring with him at a meeting. Although she would have plenty of reasons to battle Powderly over the years— for the Knights of Labor was a conservative union that

"General Master Workman" of the Knights of Labor, Terence Powderly (1849-1924) is pictured here with other nineteenth-century labor leaders, including Samuel Gompers (third from bottom on the left).

opposed strikes and Jones would become the most famous of all strike leaders—the two began a lifelong friendship.

Once Mary Jones became involved in union work, she considered her home to be "wherever there was a fight," and she was "Mother" to all workers. At the time, unions were all but illegal in the United States. Union organizers were beaten by company-hired thugs, fired on by state militias, and arrested by antiunion police departments. Court injunctions restricted organizers' right of free speech; in most states, workers could be imprisoned for even threatening a work stoppage. Participation in union activities often brought firing and *blacklisting*, a practice that kept its victims from being employed again.

Nevertheless, union organizing was on the rise. In July 1877, Mary Jones joined railroad workers on strike in Pittsburgh, Pennsylvania. Despite stable profits, several railroads, including the Pennsylvania Railroad and the Baltimore and Ohio Railroad, had cut wages. In response, railroad crews stopped working. The strike spread spontaneously to several states. State militia fired on strikers in Pittsburgh, killing 20. When the workers fought back by burning and looting company property, federal troops were called in to put down the strike. Strikers eventually returned to their jobs with wage cuts still in place.

In 1886, Jones became even more convinced of the need to fight the powers of government and industry. That year, four anarchists were hanged for a bombing in Chicago's Haymarket Square, even though there was no evidence connecting them to the crime. Labor leaders across the nation were outraged, and Jones dedicated her life to the cause of the "martyrs of the workers' struggle."

After the United Mine Workers (UMW) was founded in 1890, Jones became a roaming organizer for the union. By this time, she was already in her sixties.

Her gray hair, simple black dress, and delicate lace collar gave her a grandmotherly appearance. Called "Mother" by the miners, Mary Jones was loved for her compassion and understanding. In her speeches, she described the miners' sad lives and showed them how unions could get them better wages, decent housing, and greater opportunities for their children.

When miners were reluctant to join the union, Mother Jones could be biting. She mocked the manhood of miners who feared their bosses, telling them they

Young boys like the two shown in this photograph worked alongside men at the mines, often inhaling dangerous coal dust for 10 or 12 hours every day.

should be ashamed to face their wives. Tough and tireless, she used harsh and sometimes vulgar language to incite strikers to violence against strikebreakers and company-hired thugs. Although she was arrested many times, police were hesitant to jail a little old lady, and public officials and mine owners feared the bad publicity that would result if she were hurt or killed.

To learn about working conditions and child labor in factories, Jones briefly took jobs in a cotton mill and a rope factory in the mid-1890s. These experiences led her to conclude that "a complete overthrow of the capitalistic system" was necessary to improve workers' lives. She began selling and occasionally writing for a socialist paper, *Appeal to Reason*, and she helped to found a new socialist party, the Social Democratic Party, in 1898.

Jones went to the hilly coal-mining regions of West Virginia in 1897 for the UMW. Most miners there lived and worked in isolated company towns, where the land, homes, and all other property were owned by the employers and patrolled by private armies of guards. In West Virginia, the coal lay near the surface of the ground. Eager to keep their cost advantage over companies that had to dig deep into the ground to extract coal, the owners fiercely resisted union attempts to improve wages.

Following a nationwide strike in the summer of 1897, the UMW had reached agreements with mine owners in every state but West Virginia. Believing the low wages paid to those miners hurt unionized miners in the rest of the country, the union was determined to organize these men. The much younger organizers already sent to

West Virginia by the UMW had been unable to get past the mine owners' private guards. Jones led meetings and walkouts, but her efforts were also futile. By granting wage raises in some areas and evicting strikers from their homes in others, the companies divided the miners into rival factions and defeated the organizing drive.

The UMW's greatest success—helped considerably by Mother Jones—came in the coal fields of northeastern Pennsylvania, the source of most of the East Coast's fuel. In the autumn of 1900, Jones led an all-night, 15-mile march of thousands of miners' wives in the Panther Creek Valley. Arriving at a mine entrance the next morning with a band playing and flags waving, Jones and the women pleaded with the miners to return home. Although she was confronted by militia wielding rifles, Jones stubbornly led the group forward and soon had every mine worker on strike. Even local streetcar operators promised not to transport replacement workers.

The publicity generated by Jones's marches drew thousands more miners into the walkout. In October 1900, with their mines at a standstill, the Pennsylvania owners finally agreed to a wage increase. Meanwhile, 100,000 new members had joined the UMW.

For a short time, the UMW was the nation's largest and most successful union. UMW president John Mitchell seemed to be making progress toward the goal of a national contract for all miners who dug the hard coal used to heat millions of American homes. But when the Pennsylvania contract expired in 1902, Jones and Mitchell fell into a dispute that they never resolved.

John Mitchell (1870-1919) became president of the United Mine Workers in 1898 after successfully leading a strike of coal miners in southern Illinois.

In May 1902, Pennsylvania miners walked off their jobs. As the strike dragged on that summer, Mitchell resisted calls by miners in other regions for a sympathy strike to support the Pennsylvania miners. Always careful of the union's public image, he did not want other UMW locals to violate their own contracts. When the strike began to create coal shortages, President Theodore Roosevelt called for a meeting with mine owners and union officials. On October 20, employers finally agreed to shorten the workday to nine hours and grant a 10 percent increase in wages. But they would not recognize the UMW as the bargaining agent for the miners or grant them a written contract.

Mitchell accepted the deal, which Jones called a sell-out. Seeking to win gains for the miners step by step—as well as good publicity for the union—he wanted to cooperate with the mining companies and also with Roosevelt. Jones, on the other hand, saw union recognition by the owners as a nonnegotiable demand that was well worth further conflicts, bad press, and even violence.

The following summer, Jones targeted President Roosevelt in a widely publicized "children's crusade"—a 22-day march of young mill workers from Philadelphia to Roosevelt's Long Island home. Thousands turned up in each city along the march to hear Jones speak about the children's appalling working conditions. But the president refused to meet with her, and it would take almost 40 years to pass any effective child-labor laws.

Jones was becoming disillusioned with the UMW. Not only had Mitchell failed to push for union recognition in Pennsylvania, but, following a violent statewide strike in the summer of 1902, he had also decided to give up on Jones's beloved West Virginia miners.

The last straw was Mitchell's handling of the Cripple Creek strike in Colorado. Jones went to Colorado in the spring of 1903 to encourage miners in the northern part of the state to continue striking in support of striking miners and coal-processing workers in the southern towns of Cripple Creek and Colorado City. Worried about the potential for violence, UMW president Mitchell counseled the northern miners to reach a settlement. Furious, Jones resigned from the UMW and began working with the Western Federation of Miners (WFM), a rival union whose socialist politics more closely matched her own. It would be several years before she returned to the UMW.

In June 1905, Jones joined "Big Bill" Haywood and other WFM leaders in Chicago for the founding convention of a revolutionary new union, the Industrial Workers of the World (IWW). The IWW sought to unite all workers in a single vast union and then engineer a takeover of industry. This socialist goal was the most radical labor philosophy in the nation's history, and it met fierce resistance from corporations, politicians, and the press. Nevertheless, over the next few years, the IWW welcomed thousands of miners, farm workers, lumberjacks, and factory workers into their ranks.

Although Mother Jones gladly lent her presence and prestige to the IWW's founding, she was less interested in politics than in practical unionism. In July 1912, she returned to West Virginia, where strikers in the Kanawha Valley mines had been fighting detectives and the state militia in an all-out war for several months. In fiery speeches, Jones called on striking miners to gather their weapons to defend themselves. These words landed her in jail. Early in 1913, Jones was arrested, tried, and convicted for conspiracy to commit murder. She received a 20-year prison sentence.

West Virginia governor Henry Hatfield imposed arbitration to settle the dispute. The new contract shortened the workday to nine hours and gave workers the right to organize and shop at stores not owned by mine companies. Hatfield also commuted Jones's prison term after she had spent 85 days in custody. Much of southern

West Virginia, however, would remain nonunion and would see even worse labor trouble during the 1920s.

By now Mother Jones was a nationally known figure—a heroine to the labor movement and a bitter enemy to employers. To counteract her image as a harmless little old lady, opponents claimed she had been a prostitute in her youth. Now in her eighties, she spent much of her time traveling from one dangerous confrontation to the next for the WFM as well as for the UMW.

After rallying striking copper miners in Michigan's Upper Peninsula in August 1913, Jones headed to Colorado, where a 15-month battle was about to begin.

"These strike movements are the greatest fun in the world," exclaimed Mother Jones to 15,000 striking miners at Calumet, Michigan.

Although Colorado had progressive labor laws, they were not enforced in the southern coal-mining districts. "Rise up and strike!" Mother Jones demanded as she rallied the miners, whose demands were already part of state law. They wanted enforcement of an eight-hour day, *portal-to-portal pay* (pay for the time it took miners to get to and from their work stations inside the mines), freedom to shop where they pleased, and recognition for their union.

The violence started as soon as the strike began in late September. A month later, Governor Elias Ammons brought in the militia—supposedly to keep the peace.

Mother Jones leads one of her many marches of women and children to protest state actions.

Instead, the militia terrorized strikers. When Mother Jones was arrested in January, miners rushed to her defense. The public was outraged at the state's treatment of the 83-year-old woman. Late in April, shortly after Jones was released, public outcry was renewed by a massacre of women and children at a strikers' tent colony near Ludlow, Colorado. The possibility of civil war hovered as people learned of the deaths of 2 women and at least 12 children at the hands of the militia. But the Colorado coal strike ended in a defeat for miners when the UMW ran out of funds in December 1914. Colorado would not be widely unionized until 1933.

Mother Jones worked all over the nation in the next few years, but events in 1919 brought her back to her old haunts in West Virginia. Mining companies in the southern counties of Logan and Mingo were still fighting the UMW with evictions, strikebreakers, local police, and armies of private guards. In May 1920, a group of guards shot it out with miners in the Mingo County town of Matewan. Seven guards, two miners, and the Matewan mayor were killed.

On August 1, 1921, mine guards assassinated the popular Matewan sheriff Sid Hatfield, who had refused to evict striking miners and had even fought on their side in the Matewan incident. Mother Jones called on miners to avenge Hatfield's death. On August 20, thousands of strikers gathered to march to Mingo County to free their comrades in jail and to seek revenge. The West Virginia governor appealed for militia volunteers, artillery, and aircraft to put down the insurrection.

Mother Jones joined the marchers on August 24, but she changed her mind after seeing the state's defenses. She decided that a confrontation with the governor's militia would only result in a bloody defeat for the miners. Claiming to have a telegram from President Warren Harding that promised to investigate the dispute, she persuaded the miners to disband—although many suspected the message was phony. When the White House denied sending the telegram, Jones promptly left West Virginia.

The striking miners regrouped without Mother Jones. But the government amassed its forces against them, and the strike was crushed in late October. Miners were forced to accept wage cuts that wiped out the gains made earlier in the century.

In spite of the West Virginia defeat and her advancing age, Mother Jones lost none of her devotion to the workers. Widely popular, she spoke to strikers and political groups across the nation and wrote her autobiography. By the end of the 1920s, poor health had confined her to bed in the home of friends near Washington, D.C.

For Jones's 100th birthday on May 1, 1930, union locals throughout the country held observances, and Jones received letters and telegrams of congratulations as well as hundreds of visitors. Newsreel cameras and radio broadcasts featured Mother Jones remarking on the current state of labor relations and on American society in general. She criticized modern labor leaders, finding them greedy and lacking in dedication.

Only a few months before her death, Mother Jones was still boldly calling for change. She reserved special

*At her birthday, the century-old "hell-raiser" advised
workers to "stick together and be loyal to each other."*

scorn for John L. Lewis, the UMW president. Angry at
the union's weakness and Lewis's heavy-handed style of
governing, she supported opponents who were fighting
Lewis for control of the UMW.

Over the next few months, Mother Jones gradually
weakened, and she died on November 30. Thousands of
miners attended her funeral service at the union miners'
cemetery in Mt. Olive, Illinois, where Jones, according to
her wishes, was buried next to four miners killed during a
coal-strike riot in 1898.

Always zealous in his attempt to "organize the unorganized," John Llewellyn Lewis (1880-1969) was United Mine Workers president for decades and founder of the Congress of Industrial Organizations.

5

John L. Lewis
Labor Baron

*D*espite low pay, long hours, and dangerous conditions, mining companies in the nineteenth century had no trouble finding labor. Among the millions of impoverished immigrants who were arriving in the United States were thousands of miners. Isolated and often illiterate, they rarely caused problems for their employers.

The Welsh parents of future United Mine Workers president John Llewellyn Lewis came from just such a mining background. On February 12, 1880, Tom Lewis and his wife, Ann, celebrated the birth of John, their first son, in Lucas, Iowa. During John's childhood, the Lewis

The lights burning on the helmets of these teenage miners provided their only light as they guided the mules pulling coal cars out of the dark mines.

family moved frequently, but they were back in Lucas in 1897 when John entered the coal mines after high school.

John, who had been a star athlete and had acted in local theater productions, yearned for a more glamorous life than coal mining. Leaving home in 1901 to explore the West, he traveled by rail, hopping off in various towns to dig coal, copper, and silver.

Lewis returned to his hometown in 1906 and soon married Myrta Edith Bell, a doctor's daughter and school-teacher. When a business venture failed, Lewis made a decision that would shape the rest of his life: he would become a union organizer.

In the spring of 1908, John and Myrta moved to Panama, Illinois, a company town with a well-organized

United Mine Workers of America (UMW) union local. John's five brothers soon joined them, and helped to start a family dynasty in Local 1475. Tall and powerfully built, with an actor's booming voice, John Lewis cut an impressive figure among the miners of Panama and was soon elected president of UMW Local 1475. One year later, Lewis became a UMW District 12 agent in the Illinois capital of Springfield, where he pushed through a bill for mining safety in the wake of a 1909 disaster that had killed most of the men in a Cherry, Illinois, mine.

Samuel Gompers, the president of the American Federation of Labor (AFL), took notice of the young representative of the AFL's single largest union. In 1911, he put Lewis on the road for the AFL to unionize workers in the steel, glass, and electrical industries as well as miners.

After six successful years with the AFL, Lewis returned to his mining roots. In January 1917, UMW president John White appointed Lewis, who had helped him win the presidency, to be the UMW statistician. White soon also made Lewis the business manager of the UMW *Journal*. Lewis would use the *Journal* to trumpet the accomplishments of his allies and to cement his control of the UMW.

After White resigned in the autumn of 1917, Frank Hayes, the new president, chose Lewis as his vice-president. An alcoholic, Hayes took little interest in the daily management of the union, so Lewis became the UMW's real leader. Entrance into World War I had made industrial workers crucial for wartime production. In October 1917, Lewis negotiated an important agreement with the government that gave coal miners a substantial raise. The downside of the agreement was that they could not strike. As wartime shortages drove up the price of food, the rank and file grumbled about Lewis's pact.

The end of the war in November 1918 brought no improvement. While inflation continued to soar, coal companies were not granting better wages—and the government still banned strikes. Labor unrest swept the country and 4 million workers in many industries would be on strike by the end of 1919.

In March 1919, four months after the First World War ended, Lewis demanded a six-hour workday, a five-day workweek, and a 60 percent wage increase for miners. When employers did not accept these terms, miners went on strike on November 1. Lewis backed down when he was threatened with imprisonment for breaking the anti-strike injunction, but the government did order a smaller wage increase and further negotiations.

Although his enemies in the union accused him of collaborating with mine owners and the government, Lewis's actions during the strike raised his prestige among miners, especially after a further wage increase in August 1920 gave them the highest pay they had ever received. By that time, Lewis had been UMW president for seven months, having taken over the position on January 1, 1920, after Frank Hayes's resignation.

After a failed attempt to win the AFL presidency from the increasingly conservative Samuel Gompers in 1921, Lewis spent the next few years consolidating his power within the UMW. This was a difficult task, and

Samuel Gompers, president of the American Federation of Labor since its beginnings in 1886, had to campaign hard to defeat John Lewis for the AFL presidency in 1921.

economic suffering from a postwar depression in the mining industry didn't make it any easier. The union was divided into hundreds of small locals, each composed of miners living in a certain area or working for a single company. Locals bargained by themselves and remained largely independent of the UMW's leadership. Lewis aimed to change that by uniting the UMW locals into a single collective-bargaining force. He sought uniform contracts similar to his wartime agreement that would set wages and working conditions on a nationwide basis.

While local unions struggled to maintain membership as mines closed one after another in the 1920s, Lewis seized the opportunity to place national UMW officers in charge of the locals. He also perfected tactics to silence opposition, giving rivals plum union appointments and altering the UMW constitution to prevent his enemies from running for union offices. By 1930, Lewis would have absolute power as UMW president.

As John Lewis was making himself king of the UMW, layoffs and wage cuts sparked widespread labor unrest among desperate miners. The industry-wide depression meant the UMW would have to fight just to hold its ground. Union membership plummeted as mines closed, workers were laid off, and unions were broken. In 1924, Lewis signed an agreement to extend the union wage of $7.50 per day for another three years. But the UMW's failure to organize nonunion miners fueled opposition to Lewis within the union. Willing to use whatever tactics it took to maintain his position, Lewis called his detractors Communists and looked the other way when his supporters beat up opposition leaders.

On April 1, 1927, when the 1924 agreement expired, union miners went on strike again. As union wages in some regions fell to less than $2 a day, the UMW disappeared in many states. On the eve of the Depression, the once-proud UMW had less than 80,000 members, a loss of over 600,000 in nine years.

The UMW faced extinction in the early 1930s as millions of people lost work. Not only were mine owners pinched, but companies by the thousands also shut down, reducing demand for coal even further. In the midst of this economic gloom, some found hope in Franklin D. Roosevelt, who in his 1932 campaign for president pledged sweeping reforms to ease the effects of the

Depression. After Roosevelt's victory that November, Lewis took part in writing the promised legislation. The 1933 National Industrial Recovery Act (NRA) set a minimum wage and maximum working hours. The act also guaranteed labor unions the right to organize and bargain collectively with employers.

The NRA made it possible for workers to form unions without fear of blacklisting, violence, or court injunctions. The UMW wasted no time. Organizers traveled the hills of West Virginia and Pennsylvania, signing up miners and establishing new locals. Because many miners were defying the UMW with strikes and violence, owners turned to the union for some security against the militants. A new basic contract in 1933 set a minimum

Two years after the NRA, Senator Robert Wagner's National Labor Relations Act further guaranteed the right to organize unions and outlawed most antiunion labor practices.

wage of up to $5.63 a day, depending on the area of the country, and established a 40-hour workweek. It allowed local unions to elect the checkweighmen who weighed the coal each miner produced; the contract also set a legal ton of 2,000 pounds. (Some companies had been using "tons" of 2,200 or 2,400 pounds to reduce the money earned by workers who were paid by weight). And coal companies no longer had the right to force employees to live in company towns or shop at company stores.

Millions of laborers in other mass-production industries, such as steel, rubber, and automaking, still worked in nonunion shops. The nation's steel companies owned coal mines to provide fuel for steel production. Since steel manufacturers were not about to make it easy for steel workers to unionize, they refused to give a union contract to miners in the coal mines they owned. Consequently, Lewis saw industrial unions as the only solution for these miners and other unskilled workers.

In 1933, Lewis demanded that the AFL organize single-industry unions. William Green, Gompers's successor as AFL president, resisted out of fear that industrial unions would threaten the AFL's traditional trade unions, which were composed of workers practicing a specific craft. After the AFL rejected his proposal in 1935, Lewis met with several like-minded union presidents. In November 1935, the group formed the Committee for Industrial Organization (CIO)—later known as the Congress of Industrial Organizations—to promote industrial unions within the AFL. When Green demanded that Lewis disband the CIO, Lewis resigned his position as AFL vice-president. The UMW voted to support Lewis's efforts and withhold its AFL dues. By August 1936, the AFL had expelled all CIO unions from its ranks and a labor war was in full swing.

Arguing that industrial unionism "offers the only way to emancipation from industrial autocracy," Lewis and the other CIO members launched an organizing drive among auto, steel, and rubber workers. Thousands thronged to hear John Lewis thunder for their rights in his booming voice and flowery language.

Pleased with the administration's labor laws, Lewis (to the right of the podium) threw his strength behind President Roosevelt's 1936 reelection campaign.

The CIO didn't rename itself the Congress of Industrial Organizations until November 1938, but the split with the AFL was complete two years earlier. Lewis believed the AFL had made a serious blunder by excluding millions of industrial workers who now made up the most powerful faction of the labor movement. He foresaw the future of labor when he dedicated himself to "organizing the unorganized." The CIO's new industrial unions became a force much stronger and more politically influential than the trade unions had ever been.

The young CIO had a major battle on its hands in 1936 when General Motors (GM), the nation's largest auto manufacturer, resisted auto workers' demands for a union. By the end of the year, the CIO-supported United Auto Workers (UAW) was using a controversial new weapon known as the *sit-down strike* to win union recognition. At two Fisher Body plants in Flint, Michigan, workers simply stayed at their posts and refused to work. The well-organized strikers passed the time singing union songs like "Solidarity Forever." The union made sure they had food and were prepared to defend themselves if police stormed the factories.

GM refused to deal with union members, accusing them of trespassing and vandalism. Even though his company began to lose production and sales and President Roosevelt demanded negotiation, Alfred Sloan, the head of GM, would not meet with Lewis and the UAW leaders. The stalemate erupted into violence on January 11, 1937, when Flint police turned off the heat at Fisher Plant No. 2 and fired tear gas through the windows. In the ensuing

Automobiles sit unfinished as workers lounge on car seats at a Fisher Body plant during the Flint sit-down strike of 1937.

battle, 27 people were wounded, but the strikers held the factory. For several weeks, the waiting game continued. Then, on February 1, strikers seized the huge Chevrolet Plant No. 4, halting GM production.

As tensions escalated, Michigan governor Frank Murphy and Secretary of Labor Frances Perkins negotiated with Lewis and GM. Finally, on February 11, the company gave up. The tired but victorious strikers left the plants when GM agreed to recognize the UAW as the exclusive bargaining agent of its employees.

The victory in Flint brought a wave of new members into CIO unions and an explosion of sit-down strikes. By the middle of 1937, the CIO, with 3.5 million members, would be larger than the AFL.

But growth did not come smoothly. In March 1937, the CIO organized a steelworkers' union at the giant U.S. Steel Corporation. Smaller steel companies, however, held out against union recognition. Violence broke out during CIO strikes in late May, and the press accused union leaders of being Communists. On Memorial Day 1937, police fired on a crowd of striking workers and their families and friends who were marching toward the Republic Steel plant in Chicago. Ten marchers were killed in the confrontation.

The CIO was having other problems as well. Another economic downturn in May 1937 put 2 million people, many of them in CIO industries, out of work. Lewis turned to President Roosevelt and several formerly prolabor governors for help against the steel companies. But Roosevelt, exasperated by the strikes that were crippling the nation's important industries, responded by quoting Shakespeare's *Romeo and Juliet*, wishing "a plague on both your houses." The remark stung Lewis. He felt owners were responsible for the violence and the failed negotiations. This was the beginning of the end of a close alliance between Lewis and the president. Lewis became increasingly convinced that Roosevelt was putting business and politics before the rights of workers.

Lewis's even more strident criticism of Roosevelt's foreign policy isolated him from the labor movement.

Late in 1940, Lewis asked CIO members to vote against the president he feared would drag the nation into World War II, and he pledged to resign if Roosevelt won reelection. Despite Lewis's opposition, Roosevelt, who had ushered in the most sweeping labor legislation in history, won easily. As promised, Lewis resigned as CIO president and went back to heading the UMW. Seventeen months later, Lewis pulled his union out of the CIO.

Now focusing once again on his miners, Lewis hoped the threat of war might help him establish union shops for all employees in the coal mines operated by steel companies. These mines supplied essential coal to run steel plants, which were preparing to increase their production for the war effort.

When the steel companies turned down Lewis's demand for union shops, the miners went on strike on October 27 and refused to go back to work, even with a presidential order. On December 7, 1941, an arbitration panel awarded the UMW union shops in all mines operated by the steel companies.

That same day, Japanese fighter planes attacked Pearl Harbor, and the nation went to war. Lewis now announced he would support the war effort. In exchange for union leaders' pledge not to strike during the war, the government set up a National War Labor Board to handle labor disputes and to set wages. But as the war continued, coal miners and other workers saw food and heating prices steadily increase. The board allowed miners at four steel companies a raise of only 15 percent—not enough to offset the rising costs in remote mining towns.

Lewis had signed a no-strike pledge, but he was angry with government policies that were "rewarding and fattening industry and starving labor."

Although the union wouldn't call walkouts, unauthorized *wildcat strikes* by steel-company miners broke out in January 1943. Lewis condemned the strikes and put a stop to them by expelling the strike leaders from the UMW. But he also demanded a wage increase of $2 a day for miners and asked for portal-to-portal pay so that miners would be paid for the time they traveled to and from their stations inside the mines. When the owners refused to negotiate, a furious Lewis ignored the strike ban and threatened a nationwide work stoppage that March.

The UMW and especially John Lewis now came under heavy criticism from the press, the public, and even other labor leaders. A coal strike during wartime was seen as unpatriotic, even treasonous. Under Roosevelt's orders, the government seized the nation's coal mines.

The two sides called a truce while the government tried to negotiate a settlement. When the War Labor Board rejected the proposal, another wave of wildcat strikes broke out, involving hundreds of thousands of miners. Finally, Lewis agreed to a carefully calculated weekly wage of $57.06.

The wildcat strikes didn't stop for long. But now they were a demonstration against Lewis's tyranny in the union. For the last 10 years, delegates at every UMW convention had unsuccessfully challenged Lewis's policy of making UMW districts "provisional" in order to maintain his power to appoint leaders. Once again, Lewis eliminated a rival presidential candidate by manipulating the UMW constitution.

In January 1946, several months after the war ended, the UMW rejoined the AFL, and Lewis became an AFL vice-president. Lewis believed the UMW could not achieve its goals without the AFL's support. He fought for further wage increases as well as better vacation pay and a new health-care plan. The UMW also demanded a welfare and retirement fund that would help miners suffering from injuries or illness and provide retirement pensions to workers with at least 20 years of service. Companies would finance the fund by paying a royalty of 10¢ for each ton of coal mined.

Meanwhile, Congress reacted against the nation-wide strikes. The Taft-Hartley Act, which passed in 1947 over President Harry S. Truman's veto, outlawed union

Because of gains won by the UMW, these West Virginia miners going on lunch break in 1946 had a much higher standard of living than their fathers.

shops and placed new restrictions on organizing. It allowed employers to sue unions for damages due to actions in violation of contracts. In addition, the act banned industry-wide bargaining, and union officers were forced to sign an oath stating they were not members of the Communist Party.

The AFL was hard-pressed to fight the wave of anti-Communist sentiment that was sweeping the nation. To avoid forcing its officers to take such a loyalty oath, the federation instead passed an amendment that stripped its

94

vice-presidents, including Lewis, of their official titles. Lewis, who saw this as an act of cowardice, again took his union out of the AFL in the autumn of 1947.

UMW strikes in the late 1940s were unsuccessful in challenging the legality of the Taft-Hartley Act, but they did win some gains for the miners' welfare and pension funds. This period was the UMW's last stand in a declining industry. As companies increased pay and benefits in the 1950s to avoid union conflicts, some of the nation's miners slowly escaped the poverty, poor health, and danger that they had known for so long. Huge numbers, however, were displaced not only by the decreased demand for coal, but also by mechanization—a trend Lewis failed to fight. Much of the digging and loading that had once been done by hand was now performed more efficiently by new machinery. Only these technological advances allowed coal companies to operate at a profit as the price of coal continued to fall.

Lewis retired as UMW president in January 1960, one month shy of his eightieth birthday, but he stayed on to manage the UMW pension fund. He had spent over half a century fighting for miners and had led the effort to organize the powerful industrial unions that today still dominate the nation's manufacturing. Despite revelations of his often corrupt business dealings with mine owners and his mismanagement of the miners' pension fund in the 1960s, when he died on June 11, 1969, John L. Lewis was still revered by millions of workers.

A hero of civil rights and labor struggles, A. Philip Randolph (1889-1979) knew change did not come easily. "Freedom is never granted; it is won," he declared. "Justice is never given, it is exacted."

6

A. Philip Randolph
Service, Not Servitude

A story goes that when the powerful Pullman Palace
Car Company realized it could no longer avoid negotiating a contract with the tough-minded leader of the
Pullman porters' union, it tried another tactic. A porter
loyal to the company paid a visit to A. Philip Randolph
and offered him a blank check.

Randolph needed the money, but his union needed
him more. He would not sacrifice the Brotherhood of
Sleeping Car Porters for a bribe from the Pullman
Company. Not long after this incident, Randolph and his
porters would finally score their triumph.

Asa Philip Randolph was born on April 15, 1889, in Crescent City, Florida. In 1891, his father, the Reverend James Randolph, moved the family to Jacksonville. A minister in the African Methodist Episcopal (AME) Church, Randolph led a small congregation of about 30 people. On some Sundays, he traveled a circuit, preaching to even poorer church groups. His wife sewed and took in laundry to supplement his meager income.

From an early age, Phil and his brother, James, read the worn pages of their father's Bible. Devoted to the AME Church, which had been founded in the late 1700s by former slaves, Rev. Randolph railed against racism in his sermons and taught his sons to be proud despite Florida's "Jim Crow" laws that segregated parks, public buildings, schools, and all forms of public transportation.

Phil earned good grades in school and was a talented singer, actor, and orator. Because there was no money for a university education, he went to work to support himself after graduating from high school. A string of menial jobs—no better than the odd jobs he had as a boy—quickly discouraged him.

Randolph dreamed of a life on the stage, but Jacksonville afforded few opportunities to follow his ambition. Like many other young blacks, he also wanted to escape the racism and segregation of the South. So in 1911 he moved to Harlem in New York City, the center of African American arts and culture.

After settling in, Randolph joined a church group that discussed social issues and put on theatrical performances in Harlem churches. He also enrolled at City

College, which was free to New York City residents. In the city's renowned public libraries, he pored over the works of black writers.

Increasingly, Randolph felt drawn to the left-wing political ideas in the air at City College. With some of the more radical members of his church group, he founded a society that staged debates and lectures in Harlem. Randolph favored socialism—public ownership of all industries and businesses—and believed that by forcing employees to compete against each other for wages, capitalism fueled racism against black workers.

At the time, socialists were riding a rising tide of popularity. "Big Bill" Haywood and Eugene Debs drew

One of young Phil Randolph's favorite writers was W. E. B. Du Bois (1868-1963), whose books explored black history and social issues. Later, Randolph would oppose Du Bois's moderate ideas for reforms.

crowds of thousands to their rallies. The Industrial Workers of the World (IWW) gathered laborers from all industries into a single huge union that fought for socialist causes. Hundreds of socialist mayors and officials had been elected around the country in the early 1900s.

Randolph's work experience reinforced his radicalism. In New York, he toiled at one menial job after another, often getting fired for trying to organize unions. In 1914, he began working for an employment agency called the Brotherhood of Labor that trained southern blacks and found them jobs in the city.

After Randolph married Lucille Green, who had a successful hairdressing and cosmetics business, he was able to quit his job. He now devoted himself to studying socialism, and he joined the Socialist Party of America at the end of 1916. Randolph and his friend Chandler Owen became a familiar sight on Harlem street corners, denouncing capitalism, war, and the nation's legacy of slavery to passing crowds.

By 1917, everyone in Harlem knew Randolph, and people were impressed by his intellect, passion, and dignified manner. In January, William White, president of an all-black union called the Headwaiters and Sidewaiters Society of Greater New York, asked Randolph and Chandler Owen to start a monthly journal for the union. In the *Hotel Messenger*, Randolph and Owen promoted their socialist ideas. But soon they also exposed the corruption of New York's headwaiters, who were making big profits selling uniforms to their subordinates. As a result of this article, Randolph and Owen were fired.

With Lucille Randolph's money, the two men promptly began their own magazine, the *Messenger*, which became one of the most widely read African American journals in the country. In the *Messenger*, Randolph blasted capitalism, World War I, the government, mainstream political parties, and traditional labor unions such as the American Federation of Labor (AFL). He also now scorned W. E. B. Du Bois's National Association for the Advancement of Colored People (NAACP) because it favored reform instead of radical change in the capitalist

The segregation of the United States military in World War I infuriated Randolph. These soldiers from the 15th New York Regiment won the French medal, the Croix de Guerre, for their bravery in action.

system. The *Messenger*, which called itself "The Only Radical Negro Magazine in America," urged black workers to join the IWW. Unlike most unions belonging to the AFL, the IWW accepted minorities into its ranks.

Since the 1917 Espionage Act made it a crime to criticize participation in the war or to publicly resist the draft, federal agents raided the *Messenger*'s offices and shadowed Randolph and Owen on speaking tours. On August 4, 1918, agents arrested them at a Cleveland rally. They were lucky to be released without serving jail time.

After the war ended in November, blacks suffered a wave of racist violence. Mobs in Chicago and other cities murdered dozens of blacks as a postwar depression made competition for jobs fierce. But Randolph found few black workers heeding his call for radical unionism. Many distrusted the IWW and other white-led unions, and few were willing to join white socialist organizations. At the same time, the socialist movement was falling apart due to government repression. Like other radical magazines, the *Messenger* steadily lost subscribers and advertising.

Seeking a better way to organize blacks, Randolph and Owen began several trade unions between 1917 and 1923. They all failed. Randolph also helped to form the black labor organizations Friends of Negro Freedom and the National Brotherhood Workers of America, a proposed black federation of labor, but these groups foundered as well. In addition to this work, Randolph unsuccessfully ran as a Socialist for statewide office.

Despite these failures, the *Messenger* and his labor activities had made Randolph one of the nation's most prominent black leaders. In June 1925, Ashley Totten of the all-black Pullman Porters Athletic Association invited Randolph to organize a labor union. At first, Randolph refused because he wanted to devote his time to the *Messenger*. But he changed his mind in August, believing the 10,000 Pullman porters offered the best chance yet to spark an effective black labor movement.

The Pullman Company was one of the country's most powerful—and most antiunion—corporations. The company built and operated thousands of sleeping cars that ran overnight routes on the nation's railroads. After the Civil War, founder George Pullman had hired former slaves to work as porters in his cars.

By the 1920s, the porters rode 400 hours or 11,000 miles every month. They were also required to help prepare the train for departure and greet passengers—time for which they were not paid. Banned from most labor unions because of their race, the Pullman porters could do little to improve their lot. Any porters who attempted to organize were immediately fired.

Totten and Randolph secretly established the Brotherhood of Sleeping Car Porters in New York City. Randolph planned to demand union recognition, a $150 monthly wage—more than double the current pay—and a 240-hour work month with pay for every hour of work. For the next two years, he traveled the country to organize union locals at all major railroad hubs. By the end of 1926, there were Brotherhood groups in 16 cities. Randolph had added a new slogan to the *Messenger*'s masthead: "The Official Organ of the Brotherhood of Sleeping Car Porters."

Thousands of black maids who worked on the
Pullman sleeping cars were also organized by the
Brotherhood of Sleeping Car Porters.

Under the 1926 Railway Labor Act, management
and labor were to negotiate all disputes. A board of mediation was set up to handle emergency cases. Citing the
law, Randolph asked Pullman for a meeting. But Pullman
claimed that most of its porters had voted for the Plan of
Employee Representation, the *company union* overseen by
Pullman. The company declared that the Plan, not
Randolph's Brotherhood, represented the workers.

Randolph turned to the board of mediation. He
showed that 5,763 of the 10,875 porters—or 53 percent—
were Brotherhood members. When Pullman claimed
that 85 percent of the porters had voted for the company
union, Randolph gathered evidence that the vote had

been made under threat of firing. Still, the board failed to force Pullman to negotiate.

Out of patience, Randolph announced that the workers would go on strike on June 8, 1928. Pullman prepared by hiring replacement workers as well as security guards to protect its railroad cars. The company warned that striking porters would lose their jobs.

The union's strike vote was merely a threat. Randolph knew the Brotherhood's treasury could not withstand a long strike. Seeking advice and support, he met with William Green, president of the powerful AFL. According to Green, a strike by black workers would face strong public opposition. Moreover, Pullman could easily hire replacements. Fearing that an unsuccessful strike would break his union, Randolph called off the walkout.

Membership in the union fell sharply when Pullman fired everyone suspected of voting for the strike. Most of the porters who still had jobs were convinced Pullman was too strong to fight. Needing allies, Randolph turned to the AFL, which he had unsuccessfully tried to join in 1926. As before, the AFL-affiliated Hotel and Restaurant Employees' Alliance claimed to have jurisdiction over the porters. Because the Alliance did not accept blacks, Randolph would have to establish a segregated, all-black union that would be an auxiliary of the Alliance.

Randolph would not agree to such an arrangement, but, at William Green's suggestion, he allowed the Brotherhood to become an affiliated union under direct authority of the AFL's executive council. Although Randolph drew criticism for accepting what many black leaders saw as second-class status within the AFL, the union members supported him. At the Brotherhood's first convention in 1929, Randolph was elected president.

The Depression of the next few years hurt the union as well as the Pullman Company. In 1932, the worst year of the Depression, the Brotherhood of Sleeping Car Porters numbered only 771 members, down from a high of 11,684 in 1929. The union could no longer afford to pay salaries, and many union officials quit to search for paying jobs. Randolph's wife also lost her business, so the couple struggled just to pay their bills.

The 1932 election of Franklin D. Roosevelt was an important turning point for the Brotherhood and for the nation's struggling labor unions. The Roosevelt administration sent a flood of new legislation through Congress in an attempt to combat the effects of the Depression and to protect the rights of workers. The 1933 National Industrial Recovery Act guaranteed employees the right to select their own representatives and to bargain collectively with their employers. Another new law, the Emergency Railroad Transportation Act (ERTA), banned company unions.

Convinced that the legislation would help the Brotherhood win recognition, Randolph rallied porters to rejoin the union. They returned in droves. But a provision in the ERTA defined Pullman as a common carrier, not a railroad company, exempting the company from the ERTA's requirements. As a result of Randolph's lobbying, Congress eventually amended the ERTA in 1934 to include sleeping-car companies such as Pullman.

In company advertisements, Pullman promoted an image of its porters as black servants. Consequently, one of the union's nonnegotiable demands was "that porters be treated like men."

In response, Pullman laid off hundreds of porters and then directed porters still loyal to the company to establish the Pullman Porters Protective Association (PPPA). The company claimed that this "duly elected" body now represented its porters. The dispute over jurisdiction went to the federal board of mediation. When the board ordered an election to choose an organization to represent porters in contract disputes, Randolph and the Brotherhood won by an almost six-to-one margin. On July 1, 1935, the Brotherhood finally became the legal representative of all Pullman porters.

The first meeting of the Pullman Company and Brotherhood leaders, however, turned into a shouting match between Randolph and the Pullman representatives. Pullman had no intention of agreeing to Randolph's demands. Instead, it was counting on a court battle to uphold the company's prior exemption from the original Railway Labor Act.

When the Supreme Court decided against Pullman on March 29, 1937, the company was finally forced to the bargaining table. On August 25, 1937, the twelfth anniversary of the Brotherhood's founding, the union and Pullman agreed on a new contract—the first contract a black union had ever won with a major American corporation. The work month for porters was reduced from 400 to 240 hours and wages were increased by 30 percent.

Randolph was hailed as one of the country's foremost labor leaders. More than a union, the Brotherhood of Sleeping Car Porters was also the most important black political organization in the 1940s. And as president of

Although they still wore uniforms and responded to passengers' needs, unionized porters now demanded respect. In 1941, Randolph's union had 15,000 members.

the Brotherhood and the new National Negro Congress, a federation of political and religious groups, Randolph became the most important black leader of his time.

In December 1940, Randolph started the March on Washington movement to protest defense contractors' discrimination in hiring as well as segregation in the armed forces. While World War II raged in Europe and the nation prepared to fight against Germany and Japan, Randolph declared that 100,000 African Americans would march on Washington, D.C., on July 1, 1941.

The Roosevelt administration was alarmed. In an attempt to head off the march, the president asked the nation's defense factories to stop discriminating against black workers. New Jersey senator W. Warren Barbour offered to set up a Senate committee to investigate discrimination in defense projects and the military.

This was not enough. Randolph demanded an executive order banning all discrimination by the armed forces and defense contractors. Although Roosevelt issued an antidiscrimination order, it did not mention the military. The president did set up the Fair Employment Practices Committee to investigate complaints of racial discrimination. Satisfied, Randolph called off the march, but he still established a permanent March on Washington Committee to make sure that the government kept its promises. The committee held rallies in Chicago and New York City that were attended by thousands.

Randolph had decided not to protest segregation in the armed forces during wartime, but when President Harry S. Truman established a peacetime draft in 1947, he called for blacks to resist the draft. Facing an election in 1948, as well as a growing civil rights movement, Truman finally decided to issue an executive order banning all racial discrimination in the military.

After this success, Randolph returned to fighting racism in the AFL. Many AFL unions banned black members or segregated them into auxiliary unions. Every year since his first AFL convention in 1929, Randolph had introduced resolutions to end these practices.

Under Randolph's influence, most unions had gradually integrated their membership by the 1950s. In 1955, when Randolph became a member of the AFL's executive council, only three unions still barred blacks. But Randolph clashed with George Meany, the new AFL president, over the issue for several years. In 1964, the Brotherhood president founded the A. Philip Randolph Institute to fight discrimination in labor unions and to promote union involvement in civil rights activism.

In the 1950s and 1960s, people across the country joined the civil rights movement to seek racial equality. With the help of the Reverend Martin Luther King Jr. and others, Randolph and Bayard Rustin (a member of the first March on Washington movement) organized the March on Washington for the summer of 1963.

Randolph (second from right) joins hands with other civil rights activists, including Rev. Martin Luther King Jr. (second from left), during the 1963 March on Washington.

*At the March on Washington, A. Philip Randolph
proclaimed, "Let the nation and the world know the
meaning of our numbers. . . . We are the advance guard
of a massive moral revolution for jobs and freedom."*

At first, President John F. Kennedy resisted the march as Roosevelt had 22 years earlier, believing it might lead to violence and jeopardize important civil rights legislation then being debated in Congress. But this time the leaders of the March on Washington carried out the event as planned. By the 1960s, the majority of voters shared the ideals of Randolph's movement, and congressmen and administration officials even held receptions for Randolph and his colleagues. On August 28, 1963, more than 200,000 people gathered on the Mall stretching between the Capitol and the Lincoln Memorial. After giving an address on the steps of the memorial, Randolph introduced Dr. King, who delivered his famous "I Have a Dream" speech.

Five years later, A. Philip Randolph retired as president of the Brotherhood of Sleeping Car Porters. With the growing popularity of airplanes, few people traveled by train, and the union had only 2,000 members left in September 1968. But Randolph's legacy did not fade with the Brotherhood. In the years since his death on May 16, 1979, Randolph has continued to be honored as one of the great labor and civil rights leaders of the twentieth century, admired by nearly everyone for his dedication and scrupulous honesty.

"The first people that hire hoodlums and gangsters are employers," explained James R. Hoffa (1913-1975). "And so if you're going to stay in the business of organizing the unorganized, . . . then you better have a resistance."

7

Jimmy Hoffa
Strong-Arm Labor

The spring of 1931 was a bad time for 18-year-old Jimmy Hoffa and the rest of the warehouse crew at Detroit's Kroger Food Company. They knew they were lucky just to be employed. But every night, as they moved the heavy crates of produce, they had to bear merciless verbal attacks from their supervisor, whom they called "the Little Bastard."

Hoffa and the rest of the crew knew something had to change. Their chance came when a shipment of strawberries arrived at the dock one warm spring evening. The fruit would spoil quickly if left on the trucks. After half the crates had been unloaded, Hoffa put down his box. Immediately, the other workers followed his lead. As the Little Bastard hollered in fury, Hoffa and his coworkers quietly demanded to meet with management. Otherwise, Kroger's strawberries would rot.

The next morning, Hoffa and other leaders representing "the Strawberry Boys" demanded that Kroger recognize a new warehousemen's union. They also won a raise, improvements in working conditions, and an end to the unwarranted firings the Little Bastard so enjoyed. Jimmy Hoffa's career as a labor leader had begun.

A coal miner's son, Hoffa was born on February 14, 1913, in Brazil, Indiana. His father died when he was seven. Four years later, his mother moved her four children to Detroit, where she worked in a laundry. At the age of 14, Jimmy went to work as a stock boy. His warehouse job at Kroger Food Company, a wholesale grocery chain, was a coveted position during the Depression.

The successful strike and union organizing at Kroger prompted Hoffa and the Strawberry Boys to affiliate with the American Federation of Labor (AFL). The workers elected Hoffa vice-president of the tiny one-company union. By 1935, they had joined the Detroit Teamsters Joint Council, a federation of local unions.

The Team Drivers International Union had started in 1898 as a union of delivery drivers. In 1903, this Detroit-based union merged with its one-year-old rival, the Teamsters National Union of Chicago. The new union, the International Brotherhood of Teamsters (IBT), then moved its headquarters to Indianapolis, Indiana.

By 1933, the IBT had 125,000 members in hundreds of local unions. Through the early 1900s, the union had grown as trucks replaced horse-drawn wagons and long-distance driving replaced trains as the principal means of moving goods. The union also brought warehouse and dock workers into its ranks. In Detroit, Chicago, and other midwestern cities, Teamster unions allied in joint councils, such as the one in Detroit that included Hoffa's small union of Kroger employees.

In 1936, Hoffa turned to union work full time as a recruiter for the Detroit Teamsters Joint Council and Local 299, which represented general freight workers. Troubled by financial scandals and nearly bankrupt, the local was in *receivership*, meaning the IBT executive board had appointed someone to manage its operations. After Hoffa began recruiting workers for his new union, the local grew by several thousand members.

Hoffa took part in the bloody Detroit Teamster strike of 1937, in which police battled strikers and union leaders in the streets of the city. One reason this strike was successful was that Hoffa had already made ties with Detroit's crime bosses. Usually hired by the city's police to beat up strikers, the mob had stayed out of this conflict.

Hoffa had a passion for organizing and now spent weeks on the road signing up car-haulers who transported new cars from Detroit's factories to automobile dealers all over the country. He fought with police, strikebreakers, and thugs hired by employers. Pleased with his work, the union sent Hoffa to Minneapolis, Minnesota, to work with a charismatic Teamster leader named Farrell Dobbs.

Farrell Dobbs, a socialist who had led a successful— and violent— Teamster strike in Minneapolis in 1934, was trying to find better ways to organize long-distance drivers.

Dobbs's ideas had a strong influence on the young organizer from Detroit. By the spring of 1938, Dobbs had consolidated Teamster locals into a larger regional council that had the clout to negotiate contracts for thousands of long-distance drivers. Dobbs's Central States Drivers Council included 46 Teamster locals in 12 states.

But Dobbs was not long for the Teamsters. When he criticized the union for abandoning the owner-operators who delivered much of the nation's freight in their own trucks, Teamster president Dan Tobin planned to kick him out of the union as a supposed Communist. Dobbs quit first and joined the CIO (Congress of Industrial Organizations), the labor federation founded by John Lewis. Now the CIO became the Teamsters' number-one enemy.

Hoffa won points with Teamster leaders when he and the Strawberry Boys defeated Dobbs's CIO forces in Minneapolis. Then Hoffa took over Dobbs's old job as chairman of the Central States Drivers Council—a position he would use to rise to power in the late 1940s and early 1950s.

Back in Detroit, CIO organizers were luring away IBT members. Hoffa joined in the violent and sometimes deadly confrontation with the CIO in the city's streets and on factory loading docks. With the support of the city's Mafia families, who supplied arms and men to fight CIO organizers, the Teamsters eventually succeeded in driving the rival union out of Detroit. From then on, the Detroit Teamsters worked closely with organized crime bosses, who gained their wealth through gambling and drug-smuggling ventures. The Mafia used the union as a vehicle for *extorting*, or obtaining money from people under threat of violence, and *money-laundering*, which disguised the source of money gained from criminal activity.

Local 299 flourished as new members joined and restocked union funds. By the end of 1941, the IBT took the local out of receivership. Even though Hoffa faced his first major criminal charges in 1941 and 1942—for extorting money and for helping unionized companies put nonunion companies out of business—he remained popular with rank-and-file union members, who liked his tough-guy image. He also forged alliances with powerful union officials such as Dan Tobin. Soon Hoffa was president of Local 299, the Detroit Joint Council, and the Michigan Conference of Teamsters (which he founded), as

Jimmy Hoffa (kneeling) shoots craps on a lumber-yard picket line in 1941.

well as chairman of the Central States Drivers Council. As economic conditions improved in the postwar years, he was in a position to negotiate better wages and working conditions for drivers throughout the region.

In 1949, for example, Hoffa set up both the Michigan Conference of Teamsters Welfare Fund and the Central States Health and Welfare Fund to provide hospitalization coverage for members. He established the Central States Pension Fund, a trucker retirement plan, in 1955. Companies contributed $2 every week for each Teamster they employed so drivers with 20 years of service would be entitled to a retirement pension.

Local 299 and the Detroit Joint Council grew more powerful. Hoffa could shut a business down by preventing shipments from going in or out, and companies that refused to sign union contracts suffered mysterious bombings and fires. Owner-operators were forced to accept the terms of master contracts that Hoffa negotiated instead of setting their own rates. By the mid-1950s, Hoffa and his men had wiped out all opposition.

Hoffa helped Dave Beck of the Western Conference of Teamsters win the presidency of the IBT in 1952. In return, Beck appointed him an IBT vice-president. Beck delegated much of his authority to Hoffa, who ran the union from his offices in Detroit and Washington, D.C.

By establishing "paper locals"—locals staffed by mobsters with the power to elect leaders of regional Teamster councils—Hoffa cemented his power in the IBT. One of the most important of these mob leaders was Anthony Provenzano, a member of the Genovese crime family, who took control of Teamsters Local 560 in Union City, New Jersey, in 1958 and was later appointed an IBT vice-president.

Meanwhile, the Central States Pension Fund was growing into a huge piggy bank for the union and its leaders. Hoffa made investments in trucking companies, real estate—even in the career of a Detroit boxer. He also used union funds to create Sun Valley, a Teamster retirement colony in Florida. Union members paid $150 for Sun Valley lots, which the developer had bought with IBT funds for less than $20. Without roads, water lines, or sewer systems, however, the lots were nearly worthless.

In the 1950s, Hoffa's questionable real-estate deals and strong-arm organizing tactics drew notice from the government. In addition, many Local 299 officials, including Vice-President Frank Fitzsimmons, were indicted for bribery and extortion. Somehow, the charges never stuck. Congressional hearings repeatedly looked into Hoffa and IBT connections with the criminal underworld, but these hearings were always halted prematurely.

Finally, in 1957, a Senate committee headed by John McClellan seemed to be getting somewhere. Robert Kennedy, chief counsel to the committee, had singled out the Teamsters. Evidence against Dave Beck brought a conviction for *embezzling*, or illegally taking union funds for his own use. Anthony Provenzano was indicted for extorting money from trucking companies. Hoffa himself was arrested for bribing a government attorney to spy on the McClellan staff. A jury acquitted Hoffa even though he had been photographed handing money to the lawyer.

In August and September 1957, Kennedy spent hours grilling Hoffa before the McClellan Committee, but he got few answers. The committee reported, "If Hoffa remains unchecked he will successfully destroy the decent labor movement in the United States." Hoffa was charged with perjury for his evasive and misleading responses. But in this case and several other perjury and wiretapping cases, Hoffa escaped conviction.

Jimmy Hoffa's legal problems seemed to have no effect at all on his popularity in the union. In October 1957, delegates at the Teamsters' convention in Miami elected him to replace Beck as the IBT president by a

Greeted by 1,500 Teamsters, the new union president returns to Detroit in triumph in October 1957. Hoffa had leaked information on former leader Dave Beck to the government because he wanted the IBT presidency for himself.

three-to-one margin. But while Hoffa was on trial for a wiretapping charge in December, George Meany, president of the AFL-CIO, demanded Hoffa resign as the Teamster president. (In 1955, the American Federation of Labor had merged with Hoffa's old enemy, the CIO.) Meany and other labor leaders feared that the trials and rumors of the Teamsters' gangster associations were hurting the public perception of the labor movement. When Hoffa refused to step down, the AFL-CIO voted to expel the Teamsters from the organization's ranks.

Thus far, Hoffa had defied the attempts of Robert Kennedy and the McClellan Committee to oust him. But in 1961, John F. Kennedy, Robert Kennedy's brother, became the president of the United States. One of Kennedy's first actions was to appoint his brother attorney general. Hoffa's legal troubles began anew when Robert Kennedy's Justice Department indicted him for swindling Teamsters in the Sun Valley land deal. Kennedy went after more than 200 Teamsters during his brother's presidency and won convictions in over 100 cases.

By now, a small but growing number of Teamsters had grown disillusioned with Hoffa. Some of these opponents headed important locals and planned to protest Hoffa's actions at the 1961 Teamsters' convention. But Hoffa still ran the union as his private kingdom and locals that opposed him found themselves in receivership with their presidents fired from their posts and sometimes blacklisted by employers. Hoffa opponents were not allowed to speak at the convention, and loyal delegates reelected him president of the union by a wide margin.

Because the Teamsters controlled much of the nation's transportation, Robert F. Kennedy (1925-1968) warned, "Your life—the life of every person in the United States—is in the hands of Hoffa and his Teamsters."

The Justice Department pressed charges against the Teamster president the next year. Hoffa was accused of receiving illegal payments from a nationwide auto-hauling company through Test Fleet, a hauling company that Hoffa had set up in his wife's name. The case went to trial in Nashville, Tennessee, in October 1962. During the trial, one of Hoffa's aides contacted prosecution lawyers and claimed the Teamsters, under Hoffa's orders, were offering $10,000 bribes to members of the jury. The judge dismissed several jurors, but the remaining jury members were unable to reach a verdict. Once again, Hoffa had escaped a jail sentence.

Undeterred, the government gathered enough evidence to indict Hoffa for jury tampering in May 1963. Following John Kennedy's assassination that November, Hoffa faced his January 1964 trial with confidence, believing that with his brother's death Robert Kennedy had lost his influence. "Bobby Kennedy's just another lawyer now," he gloated. But the testimony of Hoffa's former aide Ed Partin, the government's informant, sealed the case. In March, the court found Hoffa guilty and sentenced him to 8 years in prison and a $10,000 fine. The next month, Hoffa went on trial again for taking Central States Pension Fund money for various business ventures and his own use. Another guilty verdict in July brought a 5-year sentence. In all, Hoffa faced 13 years in prison.

The Teamster president appealed his sentences all the way to the Supreme Court but failed to have the verdicts overturned. Although he gained the support of many government officials and claimed that the Justice Department had a "conspiracy" against him and the Teamsters, this time the charges against him stuck. Hoffa began serving his prison term in Pennsylvania's Lewisburg Penitentiary in March 1967, but he still kept the union firmly under his control. He remained the official Teamster president while Frank Fitzsimmons ran the Teamsters in his absence.

Owner-operators had long been unhappy with the Teamster leaders, who had intentionally undercut their ability to make a decent living. When Hoffa was imprisoned, his opponents within the union heated up their drive for change with pickets and wildcat strikes. These

Shortly before he went to prison, Hoffa (standing at right) met with Frank Fitzsimmons (standing alongside Hoffa) and other Teamster officials to plan how to run the union while he served his sentence.

factions called for reforms that would make the IBT more democratic and responsive to rank-and-file members. In the next several years, the rebellion turned into a war every bit as violent as the old Teamster battles in Detroit.

The union leadership was benefiting too much from corruption to undergo any major reforms. In the late 1960s, organized crime played an important role in the day-to-day operations of the IBT. When Fitzsimmons took over, he used the Central States Pension Fund to win the loyalty of mobsters away from Hoffa. Money from the multi-million-dollar fund went into dozens of real-estate and business loans to Mafia leaders. Teamster money also financed resorts, office buildings, and Las Vegas casinos controlled by the mob.

Fitzsimmons soon began to defy the Teamster president openly. He gave union locals more freedom to make their own decisions, ignored orders made by Hoffa from Lewisburg, and appointed one of Hoffa's enemies to the presidency of Hoffa's beloved Teamsters Local 299. Fitzsimmons also forged ties with President Richard Nixon, who was seeking the union's support for his upcoming 1972 reelection campaign.

Watching the crumbling of his empire from prison, Hoffa made an alliance with Carmine Galante, a Mafia leader. Hoffa believed Galante could help him return to the undisputed leadership of the Teamsters if and when Hoffa won a government parole. The alliance was a risky one, however. As a member of the Bonanno crime family, Galante was a bitter rival of the Genovese family, whose members—including Anthony Provenzano—had held important positions in the Teamster union and now supported Fitzsimmons.

The Nixon administration commuted Hoffa's jail sentence in December 1971. As a condition of his release, Hoffa could not run for reelection as Teamster president. To ease Fitzsimmons's concerns about a Hoffa comeback, the administration also barred Hoffa from holding any office in any union until 1980.

A low-profile loyal follower before Hoffa's imprisonment, Frank Fitzsimmons was never accepted as a leader by the Teamsters' rank-and-file members.

Beginning in 1973, however, Hoffa began appealing the restrictions on his union activities so he could return to power. Campaigning, he announced he would respond to the concerns of the owner-operators. Despite his own record of corruption, Hoffa promised to expose fraud and misuse of union funds, and he accused Fitzsimmons of ties with organized crime. In 1974, Hoffa supporters in Local 299 prepared to run for office and appoint Hoffa to a union post, which would allow him to again run for Teamster president. Two fundraising dinners were held in the summer of 1975 to raise money for his campaign.

But Hoffa's enemies demanded that he not run for the IBT presidency. On July 30, Hoffa went to meet with Anthony Provenzano and Anthony Giacalone, the Detroit Mafia leader, at the Machus Red Fox restaurant in a wealthy suburb of Detroit. Hoffa drove alone to the restaurant. After waiting impatiently for Provenzano and Giacalone, he called his wife and a friend to tell them his contacts had not shown up. Then he disappeared.

Hoffa's disappearance led to a nationwide manhunt. Although his body was never found, FBI investigators concluded that he was met at the restaurant by Chuckie O'Brien, his foster son, and driven to O'Brien's house, where he was killed by three of Anthony Provenzano's men. Despite a $300,000 reward offered by Hoffa's family and friends, no one was ever arrested for his murder.

Chuckie O'Brien denied the government's account of the crime. Unable to find witnesses willing to testify in the case, the government made no charges, and the disappearance of Jimmy Hoffa remained a mystery.

Slowly, the Teamsters seemed to step out of Hoffa's shadow. Another IBT president, Roy Williams, was convicted in December 1982 of trying to bribe a senator and became the third Teamster president to serve a jail term. In October 1987, as the movement to reform the organization began to gain strength, the Teamsters rejoined the AFL-CIO. A Justice Department suit against the union was settled in 1988, and the Teamsters agreed to be managed by a government-appointed administrator.

In 1991, the Teamsters had their first democratic election, and Ron Carey was elected their new president in a reform-oriented campaign. Five years later, Carey defeated his challenger, James Hoffa, Jimmy Hoffa's son, in the 1996 union election. The union was looking healthy again, with 1.4 million members. The next year,

Aides of Ron Carey donated Teamster funds to political groups— including the Democratic Party—which then contributed money directly to Carey's reelection campaign.

Carey triumphed in one of the most important labor actions in decades—the strike of 185,000 United Parcel Service (UPS) workers. In that strike, the Teamsters retained control of their members' pension funds and won pledges from UPS to create more full-time jobs instead of relying increasingly on part-time workers. Just after the strike's resolution in August 1997, however, Ron Carey suddenly faced questions of corruption himself. In Carey's 1996 defeat of Jimmy Hoffa's son, Carey's aides had illegally funneled union funds into his campaign. His election was invalidated, and in November 1997 he was barred from running again. The union could not seem to shake its old demons.

No one had ever created a successful farm workers union, but Cesar Chavez (1927-1993) was able to organize agricultural laborers because "when we take on a fight, we take it on to the end."

8

Cesar Chavez
Nonviolent Crusader

*W*eakened by 25 days of fasting, the union leader sat before a crowd of Filipino American and Mexican American farm workers. Their strike against table-grape growers in California's Central Valley had dragged on for months. Growers had evicted strikers from their homes and brought in strikebreakers. Striking workers had been beaten. Frustrated with the growers' brutal opposition, some men were talking about taking up arms. Their leader was dismayed. "I am convinced," he told them in a written statement at the conclusion of the fast, "that the truest act of courage, the strongest act of manliness, is to sacrifice ourselves for others in a totally nonviolent struggle for justice."

Cesar Chavez was deeply committed to the nonviolent principles of Martin Luther King Jr. and Mahatma Gandhi. To bolster the strike, Chavez pioneered another nonviolent strategy—a nationwide *boycott* of table grapes. College students, suburban housewives, Latino activists, and labor organizers joined in to defeat the grape growers by refusing to buy grapes—a breakthrough in the history of labor in the United States.

These migrant agricultural workers were the last segment of the country's labor force to be organized. Like them, Chavez had labored for years in fields and vineyards. When Cesar was born on March 31, 1927, his family had lived for half a century on an Arizona farm homesteaded by his grandfather. But in 1937, during the Depression, the entire family was forced off their land.

The Chavez family joined the army of migrant farm workers—many of whom, like the Oklahoman family in John Steinbeck's *The Grapes of Wrath*, had lost farms during the Depression and drought of the 1930s. Growers in the Southwest hired them to harvest lettuce, peas, tomatoes, grapes, and other crops. Living in shacks or tents, the poorly paid migrants followed the harvest season throughout California and other southwestern states. When Cesar was just 15, he quit school to do farm work.

Chavez returned to California after serving in World War II. In 1948, he married Helen Fabela and began farm work near Delano, California. After the couple moved to a poor Mexican neighborhood in San Jose,

134

Among the shacks of San Joaquin Valley, California, agricultural workers, a billboard advertises the film version of The Grapes of Wrath.

Chavez found his life's calling. In 1952, he met Fred Ross, a lifelong community activist who had founded the Community Service Organization (CSO) to help poor people seek better working and living conditions through civic action such as fighting police brutality, lobbying city councils for better streets, and registering voters. Chavez volunteered to help the CSO register voters in his neighborhood for the 1952 elections. Soon he was leading the drive, signing up more than 4,000 new voters.

After the CSO hired Chavez as a community organizer, Chavez established new CSO chapters throughout

California. He threw himself into this work and hoped that through the organization he would be able to do something to help migrant laborers.

Since World War II, Mexican American migrants had been competing with Mexican laborers known as *braceros*. Under a federal law intended to ease a wartime labor shortage, growers in the United States were allowed to hire *braceros* for seasonal work if they could not find American workers. In practice, while government officials looked the other way, growers illegally hired *braceros* instead of American migrants because they could pay them even lower wages. With few legal rights, *braceros* could not bargain for better wages and conditions.

Chavez knew that many growers were breaking the law and hiring only *braceros*, which made it impossible for thousands of Mexican Americans to find work. To expose this practice, in 1958 he organized Mexican Americans to apply for agricultural work in Oxnard, California. When the growers hired *braceros* instead, Chavez proved that U.S. farm workers had sought those jobs. For a brief time, Chavez's tactic worked to pressure growers to hire laborers at CSO offices and pay higher wages. But not until 1964, when the U.S. Congress put an end to the *bracero* program because of its abuses, did Mexican American migrant laborers have a fair chance to get work.

For 80 years, American labor unions from the radical Industrial Workers of the World (IWW) to the American Federation of Labor (AFL) had tried and failed to organize farm laborers. Their efforts were hampered because these workers often did not speak English, were desperately poor, and had no job security.

Labor laws usually excluded farm workers from legal protections. Growers often paid migrants less than the minimum wage, required longer hours than the law allowed for other workers, and fired them at will. There were no toilets or fresh water in the fields. Since growers housed migrants on private land, they could keep out union organizers. And they easily defeated strikes with court injunctions, claiming that any strike would destroy crops that had to be harvested at a certain time.

By the 1960s, the Agricultural Workers Organizing Committee (AWOC) of the American Federation of Labor-Congress of Industrial Organizations (AFL-CIO) claimed jurisdiction over farm laborers and had organized some Filipino migrants in California. But language differences kept migrants of different nationalities isolated from each other. Eager to help Mexican Americans, Chavez asked the CSO to begin organizing farm workers.

The urban-oriented CSO gave Chavez—then its director—little support. So, in 1962, Chavez and his coworker Dolores Huerta quit to devote themselves full time to organizing a new union. With little money or help, Chavez returned with his wife and eight small children to Delano in California's San Joaquin Valley to set up the National Farm Workers Association (NFWA).

While Helen Chavez worked in the fields to support the family, Cesar drove up and down the entire Central Valley of California, talking with migrants about the NFWA. *"La Causa"*, or "The Cause," as the movement became known, sought to improve all areas of migrants' lives. A credit union provided savings accounts and loans, and a service center helped members with work-related problems. Just months after Chavez and Huerta started the organization, the NFWA held its first convention in Fresno and unveiled the union's famous emblem—a stylized black eagle.

For several years, Chavez and Huerta built up the strength of the NFWA. In the spring of 1965, the union

The first elected officials of the NFWA (left to right): José Martinez, the first president; Dolores Huerta; Tony Orendain; and Cesar Chavez

led its first walkout. Eighty-five migrant laborers working for a rose grower south of Delano went on strike. After four days, they won a modest wage increase. The NFWA had scored a victory, but Chavez knew the rose grower was a small and relatively weak adversary. The real challenge lay in organizing employees of the huge agricultural corporations that owned the vineyards around Delano.

Led by Larry Itliong of the AWOC, Filipino grape workers in the Coachella Valley near Palm Springs voted to strike for higher wages early in the summer of 1965. After the workers there got a raise, Itliong decided to strike in the Delano area as well, and he asked Chavez and the NFWA for help. Chavez was concerned that the NFWA—with only $100 in its treasury—was not strong enough, but he decided he had to support the strike. NFWA members voted unanimously to join the walkout against grape growers.

Later, some NFWA members did not want to picket with Filipinos, but Chavez would not tolerate discrimination. He told his members that if they voted not to strike with the Filipino workers, then he would leave the NFWA for the AWOC. That ended the discussion.

Picket lines covered the hundreds of miles of roads around the vineyards. Shouting slogans, picketers encouraged the strikebreakers to stop working and join the strike. Many did.

The growers fought back by moving their laborers to different vineyards away from the roads and evicting striking workers from their homes. In sporadic violent outbursts, they sprayed picketers with pesticides and drove them off the roads. Local police and sheriff's deputies made mass arrests for breaking strike injunctions, at one point arresting 44 picketers simply for shouting "*Huelga!*" —"Strike!" After the arrests, Chavez drummed up support for the walkout at Stanford University and the University of California at Berkeley, persuading students to make donations and to march in the picket lines.

As the grape strike gained national attention, civil rights activists also joined the picketers. In addition, the International Longshoremen's and Warehousemen's Union would not load California grapes on trucks and ships. And Teamsters Union members refused to cross picket lines at a warehouse belonging to Schenley, Inc., one of the Delano-area grape growers.

Two months into the strike, Chavez tried a new strategy. He called for a nationwide boycott of all Schenley products. Volunteers fanned out across the country to pass out leaflets and carry picket signs in front of liquor and grocery stores.

Chavez also sought legislative attention. The U.S. Senate started an investigation into migrant labor, and New York senator Robert F. Kennedy became a staunch backer of the NFWA. In March 1966, to protest the farm workers' plight to the state legislature, Chavez led hundreds of union members and supporters from Delano 340 miles north to the capitol in Sacramento.

The boycott and unfavorable publicity began to cost Schenley sales, so the company finally decided to negotiate. At the California capitol, Chavez announced to a cheering crowd of 10,000 supporters that Schenley had formally recognized the NFWA as the official bargaining agent for its California grape workers. In the first contract between a grower and a union in American history, Schenley also granted a substantial wage increase and allowed the NFWA to set up a hiring hall that would replace the previous system of labor contractors.

Determined to follow up on this success, Chavez next targeted DiGiorgio, another large grower in the Delano area. But the company refused to negotiate in any way. Not easily defeated, Chavez called for a nationwide boycott of DiGiorgio's produce. The boycott was so successful that several supermarket chains stopped handling the DiGiorgio brand. After several weeks, the company gave in and agreed to hold an election in which workers would vote for a union to represent them. But DiGiorgio invited the International Brotherhood of Teamsters to Delano to compete with the NFWA.

The Teamsters were well known among employers for arranging *sweetheart contracts*. In return for recognizing the Teamsters and allowing the union to collect the dues from the workers they unionized, the corrupt union gave employers favorable contract terms.

While DiGiorgio's managers campaigned for the Teamsters during the election, Teamster members arrived in Delano to harass and threaten NFWA organizers. DiGiorgio announced an election date—June 24, 1966—without consulting the NFWA. An angry Chavez called for a boycott of the election. Afterwards, he denounced the resulting Teamster victory and declared that the picketing and boycott of DiGiorgio products would continue.

A government-appointed arbitrator mandated a new election for August 30. Shortly before the election, the NFWA and the AWOC merged to create the United Farm Workers Organizing Committee (UFWOC). The UFWOC won decisively on August 30 and became the legal bargaining agent for DiGiorgio workers.

Chavez's boycotts against nonunion grapes and other produce would continue for decades. The companies targeted by Chavez's organization, however, came up with new strategies to fight the boycotts. In 1967, when the UFWOC called for a strike and boycott against the Giumarra Vineyards Corporation, the company successfully evaded the boycott by relabeling its boxes and selling its produce under different names.

That strike remained in a deadlock for several years. By February 1968, the migrant workers were angry and frightened. Some talked of lashing out against the growers' abuses. Imploring UFWOC members to rededicate themselves to the principles of nonviolence, Chavez began a fast. Eight thousand migrant laborers attended the Catholic mass at which Chavez broke his fast 25 days later. He was too weak to speak. "To be a man," his written statement said, "is to suffer for others. God help us to be men."

The strike and boycott continued, and nonunion growers began to see a sharp drop in sales. In 1970, several table-grape companies agreed to collective bargaining with the UFWOC. Workers received raises, health benefits, greater job security, protection against pesticides, and better working conditions.

Senator Robert F. Kennedy breaks bread with Cesar Chavez to end his fast in March 1968. The first public figure to back Chavez's strikers, Kennedy called Chavez "one of the heroic figures of our time."

In late July 1970, when Giumarra and the last hold-outs finally reached an agreement with the union, the grape boycott ended. The UFWOC had won a substantial raise as well as better working and living conditions for thousands of migrant laborers in California.

But Chavez was still fighting the Teamsters in northern California's Salinas Valley. Most of the area's lettuce growers signed contracts with the Teamsters in August, just after the historic conclusion of the grape boycott. Almost immediately, 10,000 lettuce workers went on strike in protest. When they asked the UFWOC for help, Chavez called for a boycott against lettuce growers who had signed Teamster contracts.

Some of these companies could not afford a boycott. United Brands, the parent company of a Salinas Valley lettuce grower, was also the distributor of Chiquita bananas. After the UFWOC called for a boycott of the prominently labeled bananas, United Brands decided to negotiate with Chavez and not the Teamsters.

Still determined to keep their contracts, the Teamsters fought back with threats and violence against the UFWOC. In October, the Bud Antle Company, a lettuce grower that had an agreement with the Teamsters, won a court injunction against the UFWOC, and Chavez spent two weeks in jail.

In February 1972, the UFWOC signed a contract with the Coca-Cola Company, which produced and sold Minute Maid orange juice as well as soft drinks. The contract covered all of the company's citrus workers in the state of Florida. Seeing that the UFWOC had gained ground outside of California, the AFL-CIO granted a national charter to the union, which soon changed its name to the United Farm Workers of America (UFW).

Chavez's work also took him to Arizona. When Arizona passed legislation in 1972 that made it illegal for farm workers to strike or start boycotts—an indirect attack on Chavez's union—he staged a fast and led a campaign to recall the governor who signed the bill into law. The law, however, remained on the books.

Disaster hit in California the following year. The 1970 grape contracts expired in 1973, and the growers again turned to the Teamsters for a deal more to their liking. UFW membership plummeted from 80,000 to just

5,000. Thousands of workers were arrested in protest strikes and hundreds were beaten by police and guards. Chavez called off the walkout in August after the deaths of two strikers. Instead, he started a new grape boycott.

The UFW was able to rebuild its organization. In 1975, Chavez convinced the new governor of California, Jerry Brown, to pass the Agricultural Labor Relations Act, which granted farm workers the right to organize, vote in union elections, and bargain for union contracts. Over the next several years, the UFW won a majority of

Chavez rallies workers during the UFW's organizing drive in February 1976.

the hundreds of secret-ballot elections held by the state and recouped about 45,000 members. In 1977, Chavez and the Teamsters Union finally reached an agreement under which the Teamsters left the fields.

But more trouble was to come. After George Deukmejian became governor of California in 1983, enforcement of the Agricultural Labor Relations Act effectively ended, and the UFW lost much of the progress it had made. In 1984, Chavez called for a third grape boycott to protest the use of dangerous pesticides and new abuses of workers. Four years later, 61-year-old Chavez

Companies use dangerous pesticides on our food to keep production high. Focusing on the health of consumers and agricultural workers, Chavez urged people to join the long-running boycott of table grapes.

fasted for 36 days to call attention to the use of these chemicals.

Cesar Chavez was president of the UFW until he died in his sleep on April 23, 1993. His annual salary never exceeded $6,000—the lowest of any union president in the U.S. He never owned a house or a car, and he left no money in his will.

Under the leadership of Arturo Rodriguez, a son-in-law of Cesar Chavez and a UFW leader for more than 20 years, the union has made great gains. Since 1994, the UFW has won a long string of secret-ballot elections and negotiated even more new contracts with growers of wine grapes, roses, mushrooms, lettuce, and other vegetables.

Since Chavez's death, dozens of communities have named schools, streets, and parks in his honor, and the state of California celebrates his March 31 birthday as a holiday. In 1994, President Bill Clinton posthumously awarded Chavez the Medal of Freedom, the highest honor the nation bestows on a civilian. But to the modest Cesar Chavez, his greatest monument was the continuing work of the United Farm Workers.

A Glossary of Labor-Related Terms

anarchist: someone who rejects all forms of government

arbitration: a process of decision-making by a third party to determine a fair agreement for two disputing parties

blacklist: to bar someone from work by an agreement among employers

boycott: to refuse to buy goods made by or to work with products of a certain company

capitalism: an economic system in which industries are owned by individuals or corporations

collective bargaining: negotiation between employers and representatives of their workers to determine wages, hours, benefits, and working conditions

company store: a store owned by a business that sells goods to its employees

company town: a town built by a company for its employees

company union: a labor union controlled by an employer

dual union: a union that directly competes with another union for members

embezzlement: illegally taking funds from a company or organization for personal use

extortion: gaining money through threats or violence

general strike: a strike by all workers in a given industry or by all workers in many different industries

industrial union: a union that organizes all the laborers working in a single industry, such as automaking or mining

injunction: a legally binding order by a court prohibiting a certain action, such as a strike

local: a union organized in a certain location or a single company that is a member of a larger national or international union

lockout: a practice by employers of preventing workers from entering the workplace in order to pressure them to accept an employer's contract or policy

migrant farm worker: an agricultural laborer who moves from place to place to follow the seasonal harvest of crops

money-laundering: using an institution to disguise the origins of money gained through illegal activity

National Industrial Recovery Act (NRA): a law passed by Congress in 1933 that set a minimum wage and maximum working hours and also protected workers' rights to organize and bargain collectively with their employers

open shop: a workplace that employs both union and nonunion workers

picket: to carry signs protesting an employer's wages, working conditions, or refusal to recognize a union

progressive: name given to reforms in business practices and workplace safety that were enacted to protect workers, consumers, and small businesses in the early 1900s

rank-and-file members: the general membership of a union

receivership: the status of a union local when the larger union body takes control of its funds and management

sabotage: damaging equipment to prevent production

scab: a worker hired to replace another worker who is on strike

Sherman Antitrust Act: an 1890 law targeting business monopolies that was used to prevent union organizing and strikes by defining these actions as "conspiracy in restraint of trade"

sit-down strike: a strike in which laborers occupy their workplace but refuse to do their jobs

slowdown: deliberately doing work at a slower pace to interfere with the production process

socialist: someone who believes industries should be owned and controlled by the government

strike: a labor action in which workers refuse to perform their jobs

strikebreaker: a person hired to prevent or break up a strike

sweetheart contract: a labor contract advantageous to the employer, sometimes obtained through a bribe or a payoff

sympathy strike: a strike by workers in support of the cause of workers employed by another company

Taft-Hartley Act: a 1947 law that prohibited union practices such as sympathy strikes, industry-wide bargaining, and union shops, and thus greatly weakened labor unions

trade union: a union that accepts only those laborers practicing a specific skill, such as cigarmaking, ironworking, or carpentry; also known as **craft union**

union label: a tag or similar marking that identifies a product as being made by unionized workers

union shop: a place of work that only employs members of a certain union; also known as **closed shop**

wildcat strike: a strike by union members that is not authorized by union leaders

yellow-dog contract: a labor contract that bars union membership as a condition of employment

Bibliography

Alinsky, Saul. *John L. Lewis: An Unauthorized Biography.* New York: G. P. Putnam's Sons, 1949.

Anderson, Jervis. *A. Philip Randolph: A Biographical Portrait.* New York: Harcourt Brace Jovanovich, 1973.

Brommel, Bernard J. *Eugene V. Debs: Spokesman for Labor and Socialism.* Chicago: Charles H. Kerr, 1978.

Currie, Harold W. *Eugene V. Debs.* Boston: Twayne, 1976.

Davis, Daniel S. *Mr. Black Labor: The Story of A. Philip Randolph, Father of the Civil Rights Movement.* New York: E. P. Dutton, 1972.

Dubofsky, Melvyn. *"Big Bill" Haywood.* New York: St. Martin's Press, 1987.

Dubofsky, Melvyn, and Warren Van Tine. *John L. Lewis: A Biography.* New York: Quadrangle/The New York Times Book Company, 1977.

Ferriss, Susan, and Ricardo Sandoval. *The Fight in the Fields: Cesar Chavez and the Farmworkers Movement.* New York: Harcourt Brace, 1997.

Fetherling, Dale. *Mother Jones, The Miners' Angel: A Portrait.* Carbondale: Southern Illinois University Press, 1974.

Gompers, Samuel. *Seventy Years of Life and Labor.* New York: E. P. Dutton, 1957.

Griswold del Castillo, Richard, and Richard A. Garcia. *César Chávez: A Triumph of Spirit*. Norman: University of Oklahoma Press, 1995.

Hoffa, James R. *The Trials of Jimmy Hoffa: The Autobiography of James R. Hoffa*. Chicago: Henry Regnery, 1970.

Jones, Mary H. *The Autobiography of Mother Jones*. Chicago: Charles H. Kerr, 1972.

Kaufman, Stuart Bruce. *Samuel Gompers and the Origins of the American Federation of Labor, 1848-1896*. Westport, Ct.: Greenwood Press, 1973.

Mandel, Bernard. *Samuel Gompers*. Yellow Springs, Ohio: Antioch Press, 1963.

Matthiessen, Peter. *Sal Si Puedes: Cesar Chavez and the New American Revolution*. New York: Random House, 1973.

Moldea, Dan E. *The Hoffa Wars: Teamsters, Rebels, Politicians, and the Mob*. New York: Paddington Press, 1978.

Pfeffer, Paula F. *A. Philip Randolph, Pioneer of the Civil Rights Movement*. Baton Rouge: Louisiana State University Press, 1990.

Salvatore, Nick. *Eugene V. Debs: Citizen and Socialist*. Urbana: University of Illinois Press, 1982.

Sheridan, Walter. *The Fall and Rise of Jimmy Hoffa*. New York: Saturday Review Press, 1972.

Index

Central States (Teamsters):
Drivers Council, 118, 119,
120; Health and Welfare
Fund, 120; Pension Fund,
120, 121, 126, 128
Chavez, Cesar: awarded Medal
of Freedom, 147; belief of, in
nonviolence, 12, 133-134,
142; death of, 147; early years
of, 134; fasts of, 12, 133, 142,
143, 144, 147; and formation
of UFW, 12, 142; as head of
UFW, 144-147; and
organizing of migrant
workers, 132, 137-138;
support of, for striking grape
workers, 139-143; work of,
for CSO, 135-136, 137
Chavez, Helen Fabela (wife),
134, 137
checkweighmen, 86
child labor, 9, 10, 16, 20, 25, 67,
68, 71, 80
Chiquita bananas, 144
cigarmakers, 15-16; unions of,
17, 18-19, 23
Cigarmakers International
Union (CIU), 18, 19
Circuit Court of Appeals, U.S.,
61
City College, 98-99
civil rights, 96, 110, 111, 113, 140
Civil War, 103
Cleveland, Grover, 40
Clinton, Bill, 147
Coca-Cola Company, 144
collective bargaining, 11, 27, 83,
85, 106, 142
Committee for Industrial
Organization, 86-87. *See also*
Congress of Industrial
Organizations
Communist Party, 45, 94
Communists, union leaders
accused of being, 28, 84, 90,
94, 118
Community Service
Organization (CSO), 135-
136, 137
company stores, 17, 38, 86
company union, 104, 106
Congress, U.S., 20, 26, 59, 93,
106, 113, 136
Congress of Industrial
Organizations (CIO), 28-29,
78, 87, 89, 91; conflict of,
with Teamsters, 118-119,
124; formation of, 78, 86-87;
merger of, with AFL (1955),
28-29, 124; split of, with AFL
(1936), 86-87, 88; strikes of,
88-90. *See also* Committee for
Industrial Organization
Cox, James, 45
Cripple Creek mines, strike at,
50, 71
Croix de Guerre, 101

Darrow, Clarence, 53
Debs, Eugene V., 34, 51; belief
of, in industrial unions, 11,
36; death of, 45; early years
of, 33; and Great Northern
strike, 31-33, 38; as head of
American Railway Union, 9,
32-33, 36; as member of
Indiana State Legislature, 35;
prison sentences of, 40, 43-
44, 45; and Pullman strike,
39-40; as railroad worker, 33-
34; socialist beliefs of, 25, 30,
40, 99-100; as Socialist
candidate for president, 11,
41-42, 43, 44-45, 54
Democratic Party, 27, 35, 45, 131
Depression (1930s). *See* Great
Depression
depression of 1873, 18, 34
Deukmejian, George, 146
DiGiorgio, 141-142

154

Boys, 115-116, 119; prison
sentence of, 126, 127, 128; as
Teamster official, 119-121; as
Teamster organizer, 117-118
Hotel Messenger, 100
Hotel and Restaurant
Employees' Alliance, 105
Huerta, Dolores, 137, 138
Hugo, Victor, 33

immigrants, in workforce, 8, 9,
17, 18, 23, 26, 54, 55, 56, 79
industrial unions, 11, 23, 28, 36,
50-51, 54, 86, 87, 88, 95
Industrial Workers of the World
(IWW), 54-55, 57-58, 100,
102, 136; formation of, 11, 51,
72; goals of, 11, 51-52, 72;
investigation of, by federal
government, 60; strikes led by,
54-57, 59. *See also* Wobblies
injunctions, court, 25, 26, 39,
40, 66, 82, 85, 137, 140
International Longshoremen's
and Warehousemen's Union,
140
Itliong, Larry, 139

"Jim Crow" laws, 98
Jones, George (husband), 64
Jones, Mary Harris "Mother," 11,
12, 62; death of, 76-77;
disagreements of, with
Mitchell, 69, 71; as
dressmaker, 64; early years of,
63, 64; and founding of IWW,
51, 72; as organizer for UMW,
66-69, 71, 72, 73, 75; prison
sentence of, 72; as socialist, 68,
72; as speaker, 67-68, 71, 72,
76; as strike leader, 65, 69, 71,
72, 74, 75-76; work of, for
WFM, 71-72, 73
Journal (UMW), 81
Justice Department, U.S., 43,

124, 125, 126, 130

Kennedy, John F., 113, 124, 126
Kennedy, Robert, 122, 124,
125, 126, 140, 143
King, Martin Luther, Jr., 111,
113, 134
Knights of Labor, 20, 21-22, 23,
64-65
Kremlin, 47, 61
Kroger Food Company, 115-
116, 117

labels, union, 22
La Causa, 137-138
Lawrence strike, 54-56
Les Misérables, 33
Lewis, Ann (mother), 79
Lewis, John L.: alliance of, with
Franklin Roosevelt, 11, 85,
87, 90-91; belief of, in
industrial unions, 86, 87, 88;
death of, 95; early years of,
79-80; and formation of CIO,
78, 86-87, 118; as head of
UMW, 11, 77, 78, 79, 81, 82-
84, 86, 91, 92-93, 95; as
leader of CIO, 86-87, 88-89,
90, 91; as speaker, 81, 87; as
union organizer, 80-81
Lewis, Myrta Edith Bell (wife),
80
Lewis, Tom (father), 79
Little, Frank, 59
Local 144, Cigarmakers, 18
Local 299, Teamsters, 117, 119,
121, 122, 128, 129
lockouts, 26, 27-28

McClellan, John, 122
McClellan Committee, 122, 124
Mafia, 119, 128, 129. *See also*
organized crime
March on Washington:
Committee, 110; held in

156

Railway Labor Act, 1926, 104, 108

Randolph, A. Philip: as black leader, 103, 109-110, 111-113; death of, 113; early years of, 98; efforts of, to organize black workers, 102, 103; in Harlem, 98-99, 100; as head of Brotherhood of Sleeping Car Porters, 11-12, 97, 103-106, 108-109, 113; and March on Washington, 109-110, 111-112; as publisher of *Messenger*, 101-102, 103; as socialist, 99, 100, 102; work of, for civil rights, 96, 111, 113

Randolph, James (brother), 98

Randolph, James (father), 98

Randolph, Lucille Green (wife), 100, 101, 106

receivership, 117, 119

Reed, John, 47

Republican Party, 45

Republic Steel, 90

Reuther, Walter, 29

Rodriguez, Arturo, 147

Roosevelt, Franklin D., 11, 84-85, 87, 88, 90-91, 93, 106, 109-110, 113

Roosevelt, Theodore, 26, 70, 71

Ross, Fred, 135

Russian Revolution, 47

Rustin, Bayard, 111

sabotage, 51

scabs, 28, 105

Schenley, Inc., 140-141

Senate, U.S., 122, 140

service sector, nonunionized workers in, 13

Sherman Antitrust Act of 1890, 25, 26, 40

shop, 18

sit-down strike, 88, 89, 90

skilled trades, 9, 17, 19, 20, 23, 24

Sloan, Alfred, 88

slowdowns, work, 51

Social Democracy of America (SDA), 40-41

Social Democratic Party (SDP), 41, 68

Socialist Party of America (SPA), 11, 42-43, 44, 45, 54, 56, 100

socialists, 16, 25, 30, 40, 41, 42, 43, 45, 47, 49, 50, 53, 61, 68, 72, 99-100, 102, 118

"Solidarity Forever," 88

Soviet Union, 45, 61

Standard Mill, 50

steel industry, 8, 91; strikes in, 90, 92; unions in, 86, 90

Steinbeck, John, 134

Steunenberg, Frank, 52

Strasser, Adolph, 18, 19

Strawberry Boys, 115-116, 119

strikebreakers, 28, 31, 75, 117, 133, 139

strikes, 9, 13, 18, 19, 20, 28, 57, 105, 137, 139-140, 144, 145; in automobile industry, 88-89; of cigarmakers, 17, 18-19; early, 7-8; general, 20-21, 34, 36, 38, 51, 58, 59; of grape workers, 133, 134, 139-140, 142; in mines, 7, 48, 50, 52, 59, 68, 69, 70, 71, 72, 73-74, 75-76, 82, 84, 85, 91, 92, 95; prohibited during WWI, 28, 57, 81-82; Pullman, 39-40; against railroads, 31-32, 34, 35, 36, 38, 66; restriction of, by Sherman Antitrust Act, 25, 26, 40; sit-down, 88, 89, 90; sympathy, 38-39, 40, 50, 70; of Teamsters, 117, 118, 131; in textile mills, 54-55, 56-57; wildcat, 92, 93, 126

Sun Valley, 121, 124

Supreme Court, U.S., 108, 126

sweetheart contracts, 141

158

Taft-Hartley Act, 93-94, 95
Team Drivers International
Union, 116
Teamsters, International
Brotherhood of (IBT), 140;
conflict of, with CIO, 118-
119; connections of, with
organized crime, 12, 119, 122,
124, 127-128; formation of,
116; growth of, 12, 117-118;
under Hoffa, 12, 121-126;
investigation of, 122, 123; and
organizing of migrant
workers, 141-142, 143, 144,
146; reform of, 127, 129, 130;
strikes of, 13, 117, 118, 131
Teamsters Joint Council,
Detroit, 116, 117, 119, 121
Teamsters National Union, 116
Ten Days that Shook the World,
47
Test Fleet, 125
Tobin, Dan, 118, 119
Totten, Ashley, 103
trade unions, 19, 20, 21, 22, 23,
28, 50, 51, 86, 88, 102
Truman, Harry S., 93, 110

unemployment insurance, 18, 25
union membership, decline of,
12-13
union shop, 48, 91, 93, 94
United Auto Workers (UAW),
88-89
United Brands, 144
United Cigarmakers, 18
United Farm Workers of
America (UFW), 12, 144-
146, 147
United Farm Workers
Organizing Committee
(UFWOC), 142, 143, 144.
See also United Farm
Workers of America
United Mine Workers (UMW),

11, 66, 68-69, 70-71, 72, 73,
75, 77, 81, 83, 84, 87, 94;
founding of, 66; Lewis as
head of, 11, 78, 79, 81, 82-84,
85, 86, 91, 92-93, 95; strikes
of, 68, 69, 70, 82, 91, 92, 95
United Parcel Service (UPS),
13, 131
United Textile Workers, 54
unskilled workers, 8, 9, 19, 23,
28, 51; in cigar business, 16-
18; organized by IWW, 51
U.S. Steel Corporation, 90

Vigo Lodge Number 16
(Brotherhood of Locomotive
Firemen), 34

Wagner, Robert, 85
Walls and Bars, 45
Western Conference of
Teamsters, 121
Western Federation of Miners
(WFM), 48-50, 51, 52-53,
54, 71-72, 73
White, John, 81
White, William, 100
wildcat strikes, 92, 93, 126
Williams, Roy, 130, 131
Wilson, Woodrow, 27, 59, 60
Wobblies, 51, 54, 57, 58, 59, 60.
See also Industrial Workers of
the World
women, as workers: 9, 18, 20,
23, 29, 48, 51, 55, 104
World War I, 27-28, 43, 57-58,
81-82, 100, 101, 102
World War II, 12, 91, 109, 110,
134; labor unrest during, 92-
93

yellow-dog contracts, 26

ABOUT THE AUTHOR

TOM STREISSGUTH, who was born in Washington, D.C., in 1958, graduated from Yale University, where he studied history, literature, languages, and music. He has traveled widely in Europe and the Middle East and has worked as a teacher, editor, and journalist. Streissguth is also the author of The Oliver Press books *Charismatic Cult Leaders, Communications: Sending the Message, Hatemongers and Demagogues, Hoaxers and Hustlers, International Terrorists, Soviet Leaders from Lenin to Gorbachev,* and *Utopian Visionaries.* He lives in Sarasota, Florida, with his wife and two daughters.

The publisher wishes to thank Marc Grossman, United Farm Workers spokesperson and former spokesperson, press secretary, and aide to Cesar Chavez, for his careful reading of the chapter on Cesar Chavez.

Photo Credits
Photographs courtesy of: cover background, front cover (center), pp. 6, 13, 58, 104, 109, 118, Minnesota Historical Society; back cover, pp. 10, 16, 94, 101, 111, 112, 135, National Archives; pp. 8, 14, 17, 22, 27, 30, 32, 37, 41, 46, 53, 55, 59, 62, 67, 70, 77, 78, 80, 83, 85, 92, 96, 99, 114, 125, 129, 132, Library of Congress; pp. 19, 24, 65, The George Meany Memorial Archives; p. 29, AFL-CIO; pp. 35, 39, 49, Corbis-Bettmann; pp. 42, 44, Eugene V. Debs Foundation, Terre Haute, Ind.; pp. 73, 74, 123, 127, 138, 143, 145, 146, Archives of Labor and Urban Affairs, Wayne State University; pp. 87, 89, Franklin Delano Roosevelt Library; p. 107, A. Philip Randolph Institute; p. 120, Marylandia Collection, University of Maryland; p. 131, Reuters/ Peter Morgan/ Archive Photos.